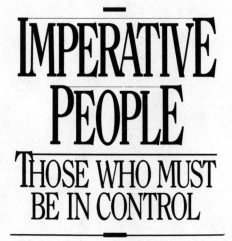

IMPERATIVE PEOPLE
PEOPLE
THOSE WHO MUST BE IN CONTROL

IMPERATIVE PEOPLE

THOSE WHO MUST BE IN CONTROL

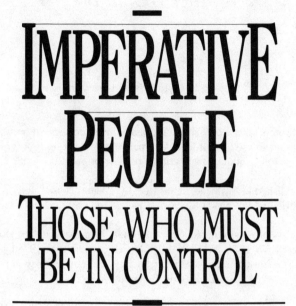

Dr. Les Carter

THOMAS NELSON PUBLISHERS
Nashville

❖ *A Janet Thoma Book* ❖

Copyright © 1991 by Dr. Les Carter

Published in Nashville, Tennessee, by Thomas Nelson, Inc., and
distributed in Canada by Lawson Falle, Ltd., Cambridge, Ontario.

Unless otherwise noted, Scripture quotations are from The Holy
Bible: NEW INTERNATIONAL VERSION. Copyright © 1978 by the
New York International Bible Society. Used by permission of
Zondervan Bible Publishers.

Scripture quotations noted NKJV are from the NEW KING JAMES
VERSION of the Bible. Copyright © 1979, 1980, 1982, Thomas
Nelson, Inc., Publishers. Used by permission.

Library of Congress Cataloging-in-Publication Data

Carter, Les.
    Imperative people / Les Carter.
        p.   cm.
    Includes bibliographical references.
    ISBN 0-8407-7489-3 (hard)
    1. Control (Psychology)—Religious aspects—Christianity.
    2. Patience—Religious aspects—Christianity.   I. Title.
BV4597.53.C62C37   1991
158'.2—dc20   90–22451
                                                    CIP

Printed in the United States of America

1 2 3 4 5 6 7 — 96 95 94 93 92 91

CONTENTS

PART FOUR: ENJOYING RELATIONSHIPS WITH OTHER PEOPLE

ACKNOWLEDGMENTS

—

Imperative People is the result of a team effort. Pam Sams has been invaluable to me in the preparation of the manuscript. She is a whiz with her computer, making my work far less complex than it might have been. But more importantly, this project became a major priority in her busy schedule. Her enthusiasm was a real boost to me throughout the time of preparation.

Janet Thoma of Thomas Nelson once again ably worked with me to fine tune the book to her high standards. She has an incredible talent and is the most effective editor I have ever labored with. Special thanks also go to Marilyn Donahue for her editorial contributions, as well as to Jennifer Farrar and her staff.

Also, thanks go to my family, Shelba and Cara, for allowing me the time to concentrate on this project. They always help me keep a healthy balance between work commitments and family time.

The illustrations used in this book are derived from actual cases from my counseling office. I have a deep respect for confidentiality needs, so I have taken liberty to change the essentials related to personal identities.

Les Carter

PART ONE

Identifying
Imperative
People

CHAPTER 1

Do You Need to Be in Control?

As Bob Wright made his way home through the city traffic, he thought, *I have got to be patient tonight with Elaine and the kids. If we have many more disruptive evenings we're just going to turn into a group of sour, unhappy people. I can't lose my cool—I just can't!*

Bob was a mid-level corporate executive in his early forties, whose appearance was always precise, his hair carefully combed to the side, his shirt neatly starched. His life creed could be easily summarized: If you have a job to do, do it right. Certainly he was consistent in his work, reliable and responsible, but for all his efforts to be outwardly precise, he was a frustrated man because of the regular upheaval in his closest relationships.

"I cannot get my wife to understand how her fussing at the children drives me crazy," he once told me. "She gripes at them about the smallest things; then she turns it all on me when I get home. I can be a patient man, but I simply don't have the capacity to live with people who handle themselves as insensibly as she sometimes does."

Most of the complaints Bob made about Elaine had an element of truth in them. In fact, he was usually quite correct in his ideas, but somehow his ability to think so precisely did not always translate into successful relational skills.

Bob stepped into the kitchen from the garage and fumbled to extract his keys from the door lock with his right hand. His left hand was loaded with files he had taken from his secretary's desk. The house seemed strangely quiet. *It's almost six o'clock,* he realized. *Usually everyone's scrambling to get dinner on the table.* Then he heard some rumbling in the laundry room. It was Elaine. Remembering his earlier thoughts about having a more pleasant evening, Bob made himself smile. "I'm home," he called out. "How's my girl?"

"Don't play Mr. Nice Guy with me. I'm not in the mood. You ought to go upstairs and have a talk with your boys. They're still mad that you won't let them go to the concert this weekend, and they've been taking it out on me ever since they got home from school. If you three want supper, you can fix it yourself."

Stay calm, Bob, he reminded himself. *Don't let this get to you. Elaine's had a bad day.* Making his way upstairs, Bob found both boys in the older one's room. Chad Wright was a self-proclaimed, sixteen-year-old gift to girls. Good-looking and athletic, he was popular at school and rarely at a loss for words. He made good grades, too, which made his parents proud. John, two years his junior, was not quite as outstanding as his brother. John could be winsome, but he was more prone to complaining, probably because he disliked living in his older brother's shadow.

"Hey, guys, what's going on up here?" Bob asked eagerly.

The boys' eyes were glued to the TV set. "Nothin'."

"Aw, I know something's going on. Have you been busy at school?"

"I guess."

"Well, I'm sure you're hungry. Want to help me get something together for supper?"

"I dunno. We're watching this show. It's about great Super Bowl games. It oughta be over soon."

Several minutes later as Bob was quietly eating a sandwich at the kitchen table, his face hidden behind the newspaper he was reading, the family made their way into the room. In spite of his good intentions, Bob had failed to create the upbeat atmosphere he so desperately desired. His self-directed instructions of patience were wearing thin as his frustration level reached a peak. With one last attempt, Bob put the paper down, smiled, and then stated to no one in particular, "Well, it may not be a gourmet's delight, but this roast beef sandwich sure tastes good. Anyone else want one?"

Silence was all he heard.

"Now just wait a minute!" he blurted. "I don't know if anyone has noticed or if anyone even cares, but I've been trying to be cheerful since I walked in the door thirty minutes ago. Yet I've been given the cold shoulder by the three people who ought to appreciate me most! If we're going to call ourselves a family, we're going to have to start acting like one. Do I make myself clear?"

Chad and John knew better than to speak. Their eyes focused on their mother, waiting to see how she would respond.

"There he goes again," she mumbled, barely audible. "Lecture two-hundred-eighty-six!"

"What did you say?"

Elaine's shoulders drooped as she spoke. "Look, you're not going to play your pity game with me tonight. You think you're the only one who's frustrated.

You're just a critical, irritable perfectionist who can't be pleased, and I'm tired of guessing what mood you'll be in next.

"You read your 'how-to' books every week, but I don't see any change in you, so until you get your act together, I'm not going to try to pretend that I'm thrilled to see you every time you walk in the room. You've got to show me more than just thirty minutes of a good mood before I can be in a good mood with you."

In their own ways, both Bob and Elaine are examples of imperative people. Each one had powerful notions regarding right and wrong. Each was so fixed on how the other *ought* to behave that personal composure was elusive. This scene repeated itself far too often.

I understood their problem all too well. For years I'd struggled with my own imperative attitudes. I felt that I'd made some improvement, and I knew the same techniques would work for the Wrights.

Imperative People

If some of Bob and Elaine's attitudes seem familiar to you also, you may have an imperative nature. The *Webster's Ninth New Collegiate Dictionary* definition of this word gives you some idea of what I mean:

1a. the will to influence the behavior of another; b. expressive of a command, entreaty, or exhortation; c. having power to control and direct.

When we think of the word *imperative,* we think of the words *control, command,* and *direct.*

A simple definition of imperative people is *those whose need for control disrupts their closest relation-*

ships. Over time imperative people lose their influence because people get tired of them. Their relationships turn sour.

Most of us have some imperative characteristics. I believe that this ability to organize and lead becomes a weakness, rather than an asset, when our imperative nature disrupts our relationships with our family, our business associates, and our friends. That's when we need to back off and learn how to keep our greatest strength from becoming our greatest weakness.

Often imperative people are so convinced of the correctness of their ways that they can barely tolerate people and events that seem contrary. Imperative people crave control, though they are not necessarily aware enough to admit it.

You might be thinking, *Sounds like the Type A personality to me.*

Yes and no. The Type A personality is driven by an incessant need to perform endless tasks for personal fulfillment. This is done at the expense of loving, accepting relationships with other people. Certainly Type A personalities are imperative people. Yet imperative thinking is not unique to this one personality type. People with all sorts of temperaments are susceptible. For instance, controlling behavior is quite common to Type B personalities, those quiet, easy-going individuals; they just express their imperative thinking differently. Often these people use "the silent treatment" to control their loved ones. And imperative behavior is not limited to people in leadership or authority positions, who often have Type A personalities.

You are probably wondering, *Am I an imperative person?* Before we go any further, I suggest that you take the following quiz.

How Imperative Am I?

Check the statements below that apply to you. Then, at the end of the quiz, I'll provide some guidelines for you to evaluate how imperative you really are.

_____ 1. "I hate to admit my weaknesses, even if they seem obvious to others."

_____ 2. "I get irritated when other people make mistakes."

_____ 3. "I tend to use words like *should, ought, must, can't* when I'm talking to other people."

_____ 4. "I tend to do an important job myself because someone else might not do it right."

_____ 5. "I'm uncomfortable with ideas that are different."

_____ 6. "I am annoyed and upset more often than I'd like to be."

_____ 7. "Once I have formulated an opinion, I don't tend to change it."

_____ 8. "I stay away from people whose opinions are different from mine."

_____ 9. "When I'm working on a project, I often become so focused that I get irritated when someone interrupts me, and I tend to snap at them."

_____ 10. "I get impatient when other people can't understand what needs to be done."

_____ 11. "I would rather let people have a false favorable impression of me rather than being open and vulnerable."

_____ 12. "When someone tells me about a personal problem, I feel I have to provide a solution."

_____ 13. "I use silence to punish those who disappoint or disagree with me."

_____ 14. "Before starting a project, I dwell on it constantly to be sure I'll do it just right."

_____ 15. "When someone else is in a foul mood, it puts me in a foul mood too."

_____ 16. "Critical thoughts come to my mind more often than I would like."

_____ 17. "When someone confronts me about my opinions or beliefs, I immediately begin to search for a rebuttal."

_____ 18. "I have a mental list of standards people should meet before I accept them."

_____ 19. "I sometimes resent having to do so much for my family."

_____ 20. "I am uncomfortable when others share very personal emotions with me."

You probably checked more than one of these statements. Each of us has enough of a desire for control to exhibit some frustration. If you checked fewer than five, either you are a very composed person, or you have a need to see yourself more positively. If you checked five or six statements, you are fairly normal. But if you checked ten or more statements, you are a candidate for unnecessary emotional stress and tension. You may be too inclined toward a need for control.

My Own Struggle with Imperative Thinking

When I encounter imperative people (and there are many in my world), I remind myself that I, too, have imperative tendencies. On more than one occasion, for example, I have said to my wife, "Let's leave the house at seven o'clock," and expected her to be ready at five minutes to seven. My desire for punctuality may have its merits, but it can also create unnecessary tension between my wife and me. Imperative tendencies can be petty!

In my doctoral training, fifteen years ago, a favorite professor of mine challenged me to develop an inner spirit that would reflect a more approachable attitude and a more accepting heart. This professor had noticed that I was quick to ferret out the underlying causes of my patients' problems, but he also saw that I was eager to implement *my* solutions, rather than allow my patients to discover these ideas through the counseling process.

"You may tend to be impatient with your clients," this professor warned me, "or you may be too critical."

"Firm principles will certainly be an advantage to you as you counsel patients," he conceded. "But, Les, I want you to remember that being loving is far more therapeutic than being correct. You'll have a powerful impact if you develop a reputation for genuine concern."

I agreed with this man's insight. I did want to convey an approachable attitude in my work, as well as in my personal life.

By the time that graduate professor gave me that advice, I had read many books about relationships. I had learned that I'm okay and you are too. I had identified the games people play and recognized the need for "encounters." I found them interesting, but none had helped me to combat my imperative thinking.

In the months that followed, this professor taught me: "People need first to believe that you are willing to let them be who they are. If you attempt to direct another person's every move, you eventually lose your effectiveness, no matter how correct you may be. Freedom for each of us to be who and what we are, that's the cornerstone of an influential life."

Little did this professor know that his words would send me on a prolonged search to understand freedom. My conservative, Christian mindset told me, "Be careful, Les. Freedom can be construed as license for irresponsibility." Yet I had seen firsthand how my grandfather's dictatorial control fed sour emotions and relational breakups in our family.

My Grandfather's Need to Control

My grandfather raised three sons in the era of the Great Depression, so he was intently focused on the "all work, no play" philosophy. My dad recalls buying his own clothes by the age of ten with the money he earned from his paper route. (I can't tell you how often I heard that story when I was a boy!) When Dad became a teenager, he moved into a job as an usher in a local theater. The bulk of his childhood was consumed by school and work, with little time for friendship with boys his age.

Dad always told me that was just as well. He would have been embarrassed, he said, to have friends come to his home. Although his mother was soft-spoken (perhaps too much so), his father was harsh and overbearing. He was king of his castle, and no one ever thought of dethroning him. In today's descriptive lingo, we would call him "a control freak."

My dad has few recollections of loving interchanges between the members of his family, but he does recall many instances of arguing and verbal abuse. Sometimes the fighting among his brothers and father became so frightening that Dad escaped to his bedroom, praying that they would leave him alone. He remembers crawling into his bed at night with a hammer clutched in his hands, just in case he might need it for defense. Strangely, the more controlling we act, the more out of control our lives become.

After my grandmother's funeral in 1973, my dad's middle brother, Oliver, took his two brothers aside and declared that he had no use for them and wanted no further contact with them. Now I realize that he had wanted to do that for years. To this day I do not know if my Uncle Oliver is dead or alive.

I also got some firsthand glimpses of my grandfather's incredibly controlling ways. (I loved him, though it was hard to tell him so.) Even as a preteen I would wonder why he had to shout or curse to coerce cooperation. Didn't he understand that people could love him more if he would say a word of kindness?

As I grew older I began to realize how his imperative mannerisms were merely a cover for deep insecurities. I began to pay extra attention to the subtle, unspoken messages that accompanied his desire for control. It soon became apparent that controlling people were not particularly accepting or trusting. Their behavior indicated a feeling of false superiority. No wonder the people they tried to control became angry and often built defensive walls to protect themselves.

Likewise, I watched people who were willing to let go of their controlling mannerisms. I found that these people could maintain strong opinions—"free" doesn't mean wishy-washy—while at the same time conveying acceptance, trust, and equality. I liked that.

I began asking myself, *What causes people to slip into controlling behavior so easily?*

When I began presenting Minirth-Meier Clinic seminars nationwide a few years ago, I included a segment in my first lecture about the effects of imperative thinking on emotional health.

I presented this material for the first time on a Friday night. The next day I overheard a person beside me at the lunch table say to a friend, "That's imperative thinking." After the next session a person standing outside the seminar room said to a person beside him, "You're an imperative thinker." By the end of that day, I heard the ultimate insight, "I'm imperative." Of all the subjects I presented that weekend, nothing attracted more comments from the audience than this one.

My lecture on imperative thinking had struck a raw nerve. *Apparently, my family isn't alone in feeling the painful after-effects of imperative thinking,* I realized. This caused me to dig further into the subject. By talking with others who either have felt controlled or have been controlling, I was finally able to develop an understanding of imperative thinking. This book is the result of that search.

The Process of Change

Now when I counsel imperative people, I work through three specific steps, which can easily be remembered by three key words:

1. Identify
2. Understand
3. Yield

Identify

During this first step I help my patients to identify their imperative thoughts and emotions. That's what we will do in the first part of this book.

Understand the Pieces of an Imperative Personality

In the second step I ask my patients to answer four questions:

- Are you driven by duty?
- Are you unconsciously dependent upon other people's opinions and emotions?
- Do you act superior, yet feel inferior?
- Do you have an inborn craving for control?

As they identify with these traits, I help them to understand how their backgrounds and their human nature have contributed to these actions. We will do this in Part Two of this book.

Yield and Be Liberated

In the final step of the counseling process, I help my patients to become committed to healthy relationships with other people. I encourage them to become liberated people, free to be who they are and free to allow other people to be who they are. We'll discuss this in Part Three. And finally I show them how this newfound freedom, both for themselves and others, will be beneficial to their marriages, their parenting, and their Christian faith (Part Four).

Imperative people can free themselves from the need to be always right. We can allow ourselves to make mistakes. We can enjoy our relationships with other people if we stop trying to dominate them. I urge you to consider getting out of the driver's seat so you can relax as a passenger for a change.

CHAPTER 2

Are You Guided by Imperative Thinking?

Within two days after the argument with Bob, Elaine Wright made her way to the Minirth-Meier Clinic in Richardson, Texas. She was a petite woman about forty years old, with blonde, short-cropped hair. She tried to smile as we first met, but it was clear to me that she was tense.

We exchanged a few opening pleasantries. Then I inquired about her problem. "You mentioned to my secretary when you made the appointment that you were becoming distant from your husband. Fill me in on some of the details."

Elaine told me that she and Bob had been married seventeen years. "Ours was a 'have-to' marriage since I was pregnant before our wedding date. We were planning on marrying anyway," she quickly added, "but that speeded up our plans."

Elaine and Bob got along fairly well in their first few years. Their sons came early, so they were busy from the beginning. As Elaine said, "Maybe we were so preoccupied in the first five or six years that we just didn't have time to argue . . . although I must admit Bob never was the kind of husband to help with household chores."

"I'm assuming the tension has increased in the past couple of years?"

"Yes, it has." Elaine sighed. "I'm not sure what it is, but I can't seem to please Bob. He's a very organized person; he even wants his home life to fit a specified game plan. I'm organized too, but not in the same things he is. He tries to make me do things his way, and when I resist he gets mad."

"So you feed each other's aggravation. Right?"

Elaine nodded. "I'm at my wit's end," she admitted. "I never know what hoops to jump through so I can keep Bob off my back. He's so picky and critical that he stays annoyed at me and the boys constantly. Every so often he goes on these binges, trying to be Mr. Perfect. Then he can't understand why it's so hard for me to just forget about our problems and put a big smile on my face, giving him the world's biggest hug."

Realizing how hungry Elaine was to feel understood, I responded, "You seem to be paralyzed when it comes to knowing how to react to Bob's ways. I'm assuming that you feel very controlled by him, which in turn makes you feel depleted in your ability to give him the love that's normal in a good marriage."

"Oh, I feel controlled all right. Bob has decided how I should think, feel, and behave. But I never know what he expects of me from one day to the next. I can't possibly read his mind. You can see how he keeps me on edge constantly!"

Later, I had a private conversation with Bob. To hear his account of their relationship, it would seem that the problems were exactly the opposite of what Elaine described. Almost in a salesman's plea, he asked, "Les, what would you do if you had to go home every evening to a tense, uptight person? My wife is unbending in her ways. She's constantly talking about how hard I am to live with, but that's just not the case. I'm a pretty easygoing guy. I don't require much from her at all. In fact, I do all sorts of helpful things that the average husband would never do, but she's so finicky that she can't be pleased. She gets in these moods over nothing at all."

I had my work cut out for me. Faced with two people, each of whom felt that the other person was controlling and critical, I was smart enough to realize that the truth lay somewhere in the middle. So I asked to see them together.

"It seems to me," I began, "that you have a home atmosphere that does not allow for differences in thought and feeling. Each of you seems convinced that the other is not living according to proper guidelines. So when you observe each other acting in ways counter to your own notions, the emotional tension flares."

Bob interjected, "You have to understand that while I do have some strong principles that I feel should be respected, I'm not unreasonable in my expectations. I mean, it's not wrong for me to expect my wife to greet me with a smile when I get home, is it? And it's not wrong for me to ask for a nonsarcastic tone of voice when she speaks. I *do* want her to abide by common-sense guidelines when she's deciding what the boys can and cannot do. But I'm a long way from being some mean-spirited hard-head who can't get along with anyone."

"Well, if you want to talk about what's correct and what's not correct, let's take a good look at your picky ways," Elaine snapped right back. "Do you think it's right to hover over me and give me unasked-for advice about my cooking? And you're so time conscious. I'm tired of you harping at me because you're worried about being three minutes late for something. You're going to have to learn that I don't respond nicely to your pushy ways. You've got to realize that the world does not have to live according to your precise specifications."

"Notice the emotions that frequently come over you," I told them. "Right now, you're each feeling frustration. And I'm sure at other times you get caught in moods of worry, irritability, resentment, futility. It seems strange, but these feelings seem to be tied to a recurring problem . . . the problem of knowing how to be correct."

"I haven't really thought about it like that before, but I know that I feel all those emotions you just mentioned," Bob admitted. "How can being correct pose such a problem?"

"Your communication is being pushed along by what I call *imperative thinking*. That is, once you are convinced about the correctness of your ideas or beliefs, you then feel permission to be commanding in your speech. It's as though the world is obliged to fall in line with your correct guidelines.

"Imperative thinking is easy to identify," I continued. "Listen for the words *should, supposed to, got to, have to, ought to, must, can't*. These are imperative words. They're dead giveaways."

"Well, I use those words all the time," said Bob.

"I guess I do too," Elaine admitted. "But I'm not nearly as bad about it as you are." Turning to me she asked, "What's so wrong about knowing what ought to be done?"

Smiling, I replied, "Technically speaking, nothing is wrong in stating what *should* be done. After all, in a world that shuns absolutes, it's refreshing to feel like you *do* stand for something. But I'd like you to look beyond the surface issues of right and wrong. I'd like you to examine the implied messages of your imperative language."

"What do you mean?" asked Bob.

"Let me give you a hypothetical situation. Suppose I invited you two to be guests in my home. And as you entered the front door, I greeted you with a legal document. This document contained twenty-five instructions telling you how you *must* behave while you're there. Now, I feel very justified in asking you to sign this agreement because I know that each item is a correct instruction derived from the Bible itself. How would you feel as I presented this list to you with the requirement of your signature?"

Both the Wrights were laughing. Bob said boldly, "You'd see nothing but my back side because I would turn and walk away. I wouldn't give you the time of day."

Elaine was more diplomatic: "Well, I might sign your document and come in, but I'd be thinking to myself that I'd never want to come back."

I agreed with them. "Yes, I imagine most people would feel that way. Now let's take this illustration further. Suppose you decided that you would humor me and sign my list of regulations. Then throughout the evening as you chatted with my wife or ate at my table, I produced the document and pointed out how you were not living up to our agreement. How would you feel then?"

Fully immersed in the analogy, the Wrights quickly responded that they would be tense, annoyed, angry, resentful, and maybe a bit worried or fearful.

"And to complete the picture, let's imagine how *I* would feel as I tried to make you adhere to my specifications. I, too, would be tense and irritated and worried. After all, it would be my job to police your actions. We'd have one lousy evening together, wouldn't we?"

The three of us shared a good laugh. Then I prodded them to analyze the scene. "Now, as absurd as this illustration may seem, I'm convinced that while imperative people may not have their list of regulations typed on a legal document to be signed, they have a mental agenda that they apply in a wide variety of circumstances. They know how others should behave, speak, and feel, and nothing else matters to them but meeting that standard. In the meantime, the relationship is lost."

Elaine spoke out, "Les, as you were giving the illustration, I could feel myself becoming tense because Bob relates to me in exactly that way. And I know that sometimes I have my own list of regulations for him. I speak that way to the boys too. And as I think about it, that's the way I was spoken to as a child. My parents and teachers were very imperative. This is a summary of my whole lifestyle!"

"It's easy to identify imperative thinking once you are aware of it," I said. "Now think about the hidden messages that accompany each imperative expectation."

"Do you mean that when I speak in the imperative style, I'm communicating a lack of acceptance?" Bob asked.

"That's exactly what I mean. You are in essence stating, 'I'll accept you only after you meet my conditions.' And since each of us responds negatively to this kind of emotional blackmail, we become angry or tense."

"Not only is there a hidden message of conditional acceptance," added Elaine, looking directly at her husband, "but I feel there is no trust or respect. It's as if you're saying, 'I don't think you can be trusted to make good decsions; you'll probably foul things up.' Then it seems that it turns into a self-fulfilling prophecy."

"That's just what's happening, Elaine," I replied. "Basically, the imperative person is stating 'If you'll fit my mold and be what I think you should be, we'll get along okay; but if you don't, I'll have to hound you until you shape up.'"

Bob was shaking his head in bewilderment. "I can easily identify many of the little things I say that come out as imperatives. But I guess I never really considered that these undercover messages came across so powerfully."

"Actually," I told him, "each one of us can admit to moments when we communicate our thoughts and feelings in an imperative manner. I'm most concerned, though, about those who are *habitually* this way. When imperative thinking is chronically used, relationships can collapse completely and emotions can get way out of control."

Seven Typical Imperative Thoughts

Because each person needs to live with some standard of right and wrong, it is healthy to adhere to solid beliefs. Yet, it is possible to take a good quality to excess, thereby creating problems. This is the problem of imperative people. They have such a need for order that they carry it too far. Interestingly, they can be wildly inconsistent. They may have very relaxed attitudes about some issues at the same time that they are dogmatic about others. Often the rules change with people and circumstances.

I find that imperative people are easily identified by seven typical imperative thoughts. During the first step of counseling I help my patients to identify their imperative thoughts and emotions. We will look at the seven typical imperative thoughts in this chapter. And then in chapter 3 we will look at the emotions that often drive these thoughts.

1. *"I Emphasize Performance Over Relationships."*

Have you ever realized that achievements can take priority over people? For instance, would you rather finish a project than spend time listening to a family member? If so, you might be an imperative person.

Remember the statement, "When I'm working on a project, I often become so focused that I get irritated when someone interrupts me, and I tend to snap at them," from the quiz in the first chapter. Did you check that statement? I often use these statements in my initial evaluation of a patient, since seven of the statements in that quiz are directly related to the performance mindset of imperative persons.

Most of us are aware that a truly successful person must be able to relate to other people in loving, accepting ways. Yet this belief is often rejected in American corporations where performance is more important than interpersonal skills.

Bob Wright admitted to me, "I know at work I get a real tunnel vision regarding my daily demands. The phone rings constantly, and in between I have reports to write and meetings to organize."

I asked, "So how does this affect your relationships with your associates?"

"Oh, sometimes I'm a real bear and I don't even realize it. I've been known to snap at a coworker because I just had to get a job completed. Or I have ignored people who are trying to inject a moment of lightheartedness into the atmosphere. Nothing else matters beyond doing what's supposed to be done."

"What about at home? Does this tendency ever carry over?"

"Yeah, I hate to admit it, but it does. Last Saturday my two boys and I were doing yard work when Chad stopped to talk with a couple of friends who came wandering by. I didn't fuss at him like I wanted to, but I remember thinking that he shouldn't be goofing off until he finished his work. I was really getting irked, even though he was just doing what any other sixteen-year-old kid would do."

"It seems that once you get your agenda mentally fixed, others' needs or feelings become secondary," I pointed out. "You may succeed in getting your work completed, but it comes at the expense of hurting personal relationships."

"Yeah, Elaine tells me that I should be less concerned about getting everything organized to meet my standards so I can appreciate personal things more. I know she's right, but it seems like something in me just can't tolerate uncompleted tasks."

Like most imperative people, Bob was more interested in completing a job successfully than in his relationship with fellow employees. He was bound to be frustrated when some of the people in his company either had different performance goals or placed more emphasis on interpersonal relationships and would not conform to his plans.

2. *"I'm Uncomfortable with Ideas That Are Different from Mine."*

A typical direct or indirect admission an imperative person will make to me in counseling is, "I'm uncomfortable with someone whose ideas are different from mine."

For instance, after a particularly frustrating week, Elaine Wright was in a mood to unload her tensions in my office. "Bob and I are so completely opposite that we'll never be able to get along! When I think the boys should have one curfew, he thinks it ought to be something else. I'll want to have friends over on Friday nights, and he wants to watch TV. I like to listen to tapes; he'd rather read. We're so far apart in so many little things that we can't seem to resolve problems without an argument."

"I'm sure that someone in your past has advised you just to accept the fact that you and Bob are different. How do you respond when you hear that?" I asked.

"I don't like it. I mean, I know it's the right thing to do, but how far can a person be stretched? I just wish my husband could be as cooperative and sensitive as some of the other men I know. We'd have a lot fewer problems."

Was Elaine wrong to desire close compatibility with Bob? I don't think so. Any relationship is smoother when two people enjoy similar lifestyles. But by wishing for (actually insisting on) a sameness that simply did not exist, Elaine was setting herself up for unnecessary tensions. First, she was failing to acknowledge the benefits of a husband and wife having different strengths. Second, by focusing so harshly on their differences Elaine was overlooking or minimizing their areas of compatibility. Finally, she was discounting her own strength to handle problems, and she was falsely assuming that she—and only she—would have to deal with the situation. She was not trusting either Bob or God to help her.

Insecurity causes us to have a low tolerance for differing ideas or opinions because they seem to be a threat to our authority or validity. We sense that differentness will require us to step away from our comfort zones, potentially exposing our weaknesses.

SEVEN IMPERATIVE THOUGHTS

1. "I emphasize performance over relationships."

2. "I'm uncomfortable with ideas that are different from mine."

3. "I try to control as much of my life as possible."

4. "I often feel driven to do something because it's my duty."

5. "It is difficult for me to admit my weaknesses."

6. "I don't like my emotions—or other people's emotions—to get out of control."

7. "I get irritated when other people make mistakes."

3. *"I Try to Control As Much of My Life As Possible."*

We hold the false notion that the best way to find personal satisfaction is to control as much of our world as we can. Often, we do not openly admit this belief because it makes us appear too overbearing, but our many daily efforts to control another person's behavior indicate that this is a firmly held belief.

As Elaine was complaining about her areas of disagreement with Bob, I asked her, "When you are aware that your husband is acting in ways contrary to your beliefs, what do you do?"

Smiling sheepishly, as if she had been caught, Elaine offered, "Oh, I've been known to go for quite some time without speaking to him. Or sometimes I get real fed up and start telling him how he ought to change. My response depends on the circumstances."

"It sounds like it's easy to resort to control tactics."

She responded a bit defensively: "Yeah, maybe. But if I'm somewhat controlling, then Bob is the master controller because he *has* to have things his way."

A cornerstone trait of the imperative person is the *need* to be in control. We try to tell ourselves that this is leadership, but the tactics we use show that we will be content only when we maintain a superior hand over others. These tactics are destructive to healthy interactions since none of us were created to constantly dominate other human beings.

Many of our control practices are very obvious. We all recognize manipulations like bossiness, shouting, butting in on another person's tasks, and giving unsolicited advice. And we are aware of those key words: *should, ought, must,* and *can't.*

At other times the control tactics can be quite subtle.

Negative responses such as withdrawal, ignoring advice, procrastinating, giving weak excuses, or being quietly uncooperative are just as manipulative. If you checked the quiz statement "I use silence to respond to those who disappoint or disagree with me," you use subtle control tactics. The common thread in all controlling behaviors is the preservation of oneself at the expense of the other person; the need to be dominant supersedes any other concern.

4. *"I Often Feel Driven to Do Something Because It's My Duty."*

There is a fine distinction between commitment and obligation. Commitment implies a freely chosen plan, which may at times require self-restricting decisions. Obligation, however, often implies a forced activity, which is fulfilled against the will. Imperative people have a way of turning commitments into obligations, which creates feelings of resentment in themselves and in others. If you checked the quiz statement, "I sometimes resent having to do so much for my family," you are operating from obligation, not commitment.

The first time I met with Elaine, as I heard her describe how frustrated she was with Bob and saw how she regularly added to their problems with angry responses, I asked her, "What causes you to stay with him?"

Her answer was another clue to her imperative personality: "I *have* to."

When we are locked into imperative thinking, we hold our absolute convictions so tightly that we have little or no recognition of our choice to say *no!* Obligation becomes our driving force. Relationships with other people and our responsibilities to them then become matters of dread, resentment, and guilt.

Our need for a structured, orderly life can be so powerful that we refuse to make allowance for choices. To us, circumstances are either black or white. Once we settle upon a conviction or preference, we feel rigidly obligated to abide by it, with little variation.

I posed a question to Elaine: "Let's say you had regular contact with someone very kind and friendly. You would, no doubt, feel a real attraction to her. But then let's suppose that you overheard a conversation in which this friend said she was being kind to you only because she felt obliged to act that way. How would you feel?"

Knowing where the conversation was going, she responded, "I would be hurt and disappointed."

"In other words, you would only want to receive her kindness if you knew it was genuine. Obligatory kindness does nothing to stimulate real closeness."

"I see what you mean," she said. "I can be conscientious, but I don't have to feel forced to do something."

Imperative people are almost afraid to allow for the luxury of choices. We feel the need to minimize our risks by sticking to the rules that we have made for ourselves.

5. *"It Is Difficult for Me to Admit My Weaknesses."*

Do people sometimes tease you by saying, "You know, you are never wrong"? If so, you are probably an imperative person who is threatened by admitting any personal flaws. You probably checked the quiz statements "I hate to admit my weaknesses, even if they seem obvious to others" and "I feel that I shouldn't make mistakes."

No one who is trying to write an ideal script for his or her life will want to include the ugly side of his nature.

Most of us have a natural inclination to gloss over our weaknesses. However, imperative people go one step further. They want everyone to see them as having no flaws at all.

Bob and Elaine were in a particularly combative mood during one joint visit to my office. As usual neither one of them was willing to admit to any flaws. In low, grumbling tones Bob said to Elaine, "The problem with you is that you just can't accept me (or anyone else) for what I am. You're too rigid."

Elaine defended herself quickly. "Do you want to talk about rigid? What about your discipline style with the boys? You know you're too hard on them. They complain to me constantly about the latest restriction you've put on them."

Not to be outdone, Bob retorted, "I don't think you're going to win any medals for 'Mother of the Year.' You may not be as openly irritated with the boys, but you've been known to give the silent treatment to the whole family."

"Bob, I just wish for once you would quit taking jabs at me. You're no saint, but I feel as if you expect me to be perfect before we can really get along well."

I interjected, "Out of curiosity, when was the last time either one of you said, 'You're right, when the other one confronted you with a weakness?"

Both Wrights chuckled sheepishly. They didn't have to say a word for me to know the answer.

"It seems that you each have a powerful need to point out the other's shortcomings, but there is little willingness to openly consider your own. I would think that the admission of personal failings would go a long way toward easing the tension in your house."

Bob and Elaine both admitted that it was unnatural to say, "I made a mistake" or "You've made a good point."

To do so would require stepping out of the driver's seat into the less comfortable position of vulnerability.

6. *"I Don't Like My Emotions—or Other People's Emotions—to Get Out of Control."*

Emotions are not always logical (and therefore are difficult to predict) since they represent the subjective part of our personalities. Yet despite the impossibility of maintaining tight control over emotions, imperative people wish to do exactly that. We may realize (on either a conscious or a subconscious level) that we need to be flexible and patient when other people are angry or upset, but this is bothersome to us since our natural bent is to neatly resolve any matters that create discomfort.

If you checked the statement, "I am uncomfortable when others share very personal emotions with me," you tend to have an imperative personality.

Privately, Bob told me of the irritability he felt when Elaine wouldn't "let go of one of her moods." Leaning toward me, he complained, "I know a woman's going to be more emotionally charged than a man. They're just wired differently. But how much of her erratic nature do I have to accept? Good grief! She can talk about feelings for hours. I'm the kind of guy that likes to get to the point. If you're feeling sad or annoyed or worried, fine. I can handle the fact that you're going to have emotions. But don't just sit there and talk about it; *do something.*"

"I'm sure when you've shared this philosophy with Elaine, she became even more upset."

"You got that right, Les. She just expects me to let her ramble on and on."

Bob was overlooking the fact that each person will experience a broad array of emotions, ranging from the very pleasant to the very distasteful. Our feelings should not be the guiding force of our lives, but they should not be bottled up and contained. Rather than requiring machinelike precision from each other, we need to allow others to express their emotions.

7. *"I Get Irritated When Other People Make Mistakes."*

The imperative person has very idealistic expectations. Only the best is acceptable. Frailties, common to our humanness, are despised. The result is a strong tendency to look upon anything less than ideal with disdain. That's why imperative people often admit, "I get irritated when other people make mistakes." Or "I tend to do an important job myself because someone else might not do it right." Or "I get impatient when other people can't understand what needs to be done."

"I've got to admit," Bob told me, "that my most tormenting personal trait is my tendency to criticize others. I don't really want to be that way, but it drives me nuts when I see people doing dumb things at work, at church, at social gatherings."

"So critical thoughts, then, dominate your mind."

"They sure do. And what's worse, I usually have plenty of critical things to *say*. Elaine has scolded me more than a few times about how I expect too much from others."

Smiling I stated, "It sounds odd for me to say this, but in some respects you'd be a lot more composed if you knew less about right and wrong. At least you wouldn't have so many reasons to find fault."

Bob nodded in agreement. He knew exactly what I meant.

Imperative people find it impossible to be true to their beliefs and also accept other people's beliefs and choices. We assume that accepting a person with ideas that we consider wrong is the same as condoning that wrong. So, clutching onto our high ideals, we tend to hold ourselves above others. False superiority is felt. Condemnation is communicated. Annoyance is a constant companion. Relationships suffer. Nonetheless, the imperative person *must* cling to correctness.

If you identified with three or four of these seven traits, you have a tendency to be imperative, just as I do. By identifying these seven types of imperative thinking, we can become aware of the variety of tensions that accompany them.

Bob and Elaine each clung to dogmatic notions that eventually damaged their marital relationship. As we examined the ways their imperative thinking was manifested, their curiosity was pricked. They became motivated to understand more fully the reasons for their feelings.

Elaine stated, "I've always known something was not right in my approach to personal issues, but I've never been able to exactly put my finger on it. Now that I understand my imperative thinking patterns, I have a much clearer idea of how I'm causing some of my own grief."

"Often your emotions are controlling your actions, although you don't realize it," I told the Wrights. I suggested that we examine the emotional repercussions of their imperative thinking—anger and fear, false guilt and worry—in our next sessions.

We'll do that in the next chapter.

CHAPTER 3

Do Your Emotions Control Your Actions?

Imperative people. Those who must be in control. Let's modify that description to correspond to reality: those who think they are in control. Often the world is not as imperative people think it is. Often they lie to themselves without realizing it. They *think* they are in control. In reality *their emotions are controlling them*. And those emotions are driven by their imperative thinking. These people can be helped by an understanding of how this type of thinking makes their emotions go awry to harm themselves and others. That's how I begin to work with my patients, and that's how I began counseling the Wrights.

"The emotions you are feeling are indicative of a controlling nature," I told Bob and Elaine Wright during one of their joint sessions. "Four emotions—anger, fear, worry, and false guilt—indicate we are trying to control others. Most of us experience these emotions at one time or another, but someone who is controlling is likely to experience them more often."

"I'll be honest with you. I really don't think much about my emotions," Bob admitted. "My family never really talked about feelings when I grew up. I'll need some coaching."

"You're not alone in that respect," I responded. "Many people have been raised in families where the proper performance—typified by the old adage 'Children should be seen and not heard'—was more important than a child's being able to express his or her emotions. Before we can change that, we need to take some time to understand why we feel the way we do. Whether we acknowledge our emotions or not, they are an integral part of who we are."

My goal at this point in the Wrights' therapy was to help them see the connection between their imperative thoughts and their disruptive emotions. After developing this awareness, the Wrights would be ready to "go beneath the surface" to determine why they felt as they did.

Anger

No person can live in this world without being angry at times. This emotion is a natural reaction, in which we stand up for our self-respect, our personal needs, and our deeply held convictions. Since certain negative situations call for us to take a firm stand for what is right, it is harmful to never express anger.

Problems arise, however, when normal anger leads to resentment and bitterness. For example, if a man is persistently inconsiderate of me, I have a couple of choices. I can express my displeasure about this to him and suggest ways for us to get along better. Once I've expressed my anger, I can choose to forgive his errors. That's an example of normal anger. However, if I cling to my desire for this man to be as I tell him to be and think about this over and over again in my mind, I set myself up for bouts of ugly resentment and bitterness. My imperative mindset has pushed my legitimate anger to an unhealthy level.

I shared these thoughts with Bob, then prompted him to analyze his own anger. "Bob, think about that evening when you came home and tried to get along with your wife and kids, then felt so frustrated because it seemed impossible. Your initial anger was legitimate, but as you pushed yourself to be the picture of perfect composure, you were probably nursing the imperative thought: *Elaine had better respond well to my efforts!*"

Bob slowly nodded his head. "Yeah, I *was* angry," he said. "After all, I was pulling out all the stops, trying to show Elaine that I wanted to be friends, but she wasn't cooperating. That really made me mad!"

"That anger didn't come from nowhere," I explained. "It's a natural extension of imperative thinking. If you had not expected Elaine to respond as you demanded, your anger never would have gotten out of control. You can only be responsible for your own actions, not someone else's."

Turning to Elaine, I asked, "Do you become angry very often, even though you don't show it?"

"Well, not really. I don't think I have any real deep anger," she said. "I just get frustrated and maybe a little irritated."

"You don't raise your voice very often, and you don't slam doors. Right?"

Elaine nodded her agreement.

"But you still get angry, deep down inside. Remember, you don't have to yell or raise a ruckus to be angry. When you're feeling frustrated or annoyed or irritated, that's anger—it's just not out of control yet."

"Well, if frustration is anger, then I have to plead guilty," Elaine admitted.

"Now go back to that same evening. What were you thinking as you became more and more frustrated?

"I guess I was thinking, *If Bob would only stop being a Dr. Jeckyll and Mr. Hyde. If he'd just change, everything would be all right again.*"

"That's not much different from what Bob was thinking. Each of you was expecting the other to respond as you wanted. That's imperative thinking."

How About You?

Now that you've seen how imperative thinking contributed to the Wrights' anger, look at yourself. Check the statements that apply to you in the quiz below.

1. ____ "I become irritated about petty matters and nonessential issues."
2. ____ "When people annoy me, I punish them by giving them the silent treatment."
3. ____ "I often procrastinate to get back at someone who is trying to tell me what to do."
4. ____ "I sometimes use a pleading tone of voice to get others to do things my way."
5. ____ "I think about an unpleasant experience over and over again, feeling that the other person shouldn't have responded that way."
6. ____ "I use sarcasm or humor to disguise how upset I am by some issues or experiences."
7. ____ "I sometimes state my convictions in ways that may seem harsh to other people—and even critical of them."
8. ____ "I sometimes hold grudges."
9. ____ "When someone asks me to do something I don't want to do, I only make a halfhearted effort."

10. _____ "I tend to do what I want to do, whether or not it will have an ill effect on the people around me."

Since normal anger can cause anyone to feel this way, every one of us will see ourselves in a couple of these statements. However, if you checked five of the above statements, the purpose of your anger is to establish unhealthy control over others. You are unconsciously thinking, "I want my world to go my way." Sometimes this anger will result in a temporary sense of control, but over a period of time this imperative attitude will cause other people to rebel. And you won't feel any real satisfaction because you will realize that your emotional energy has been wasted.

For example, Elaine told me, "I get really annoyed with Bob because sometimes he is very pleasant and other times he is cranky or aloof. I get tired of guessing what mood to expect."

"Your annoyance has a normal beginning," I admitted. "The danger comes when you think, _He's got to be consistent_. The truth is, _He doesn't have to be anything_."

In counseling I emphasize, "Everyone is responsible for his or her own emotions, just as everyone is responsible for his or her own actions." Imperative people can change the thoughts and emotions that control their actions.

For example, a parent may legitimately want a child to keep his or her room clean. The parent feels frustrated when the child is sloppy. The parent has two options. The parent can choose to be imperative, "You'd better get that room cleaned now!" which will only increase the tension between the two of them. Or the parent can say firmly, "Your room is dirty and needs to be cleaned. If it's not clean by this afternoon, you'll lose telephone privileges." Obviously the parent's voice as well as his or her words contribute to the interaction. Even the words "I love you" don't convey love and acceptance if they are spoken in the tone a drill sergeant uses to command his troops.

Fear

I have found that most people do not openly admit the extent of their fearfulness—to themselves or to others. Instead we become defensive and turn our fearfulness into accusations. "It's all *your* fault," we cry.

I pointed this out to Bob and Elaine Wright; then I asked them, "Can you see how you are attempting to control each other by being guarded and calculated?"

Both of them nodded in agreement. But Bob had a reservation. "What if my fears are true? Sometimes I feel as if I can't trust Elaine. I'm defensive because I'm afraid she'll use my disclosures against me."

"I understand how you feel," I replied. "I guess people have been defensive ever since Adam and Eve began blaming each other for their problems. Also I know that no family is perfect. Some of us have had too many painful experiences that have taught us to be very cautious."

"So it's normal to be defensive sometimes?"

"Yes, as long as it doesn't become a debilitating habit. From what you and Elaine are telling me, however, I suspect that each of you interprets the other's defensiveness as an unwillingness to be cooperative.

"That's the way we all tend to interpret defensive behavior," I told the Wrights. "It will help you to slow your defensive behavior if you realize that denial, evasiveness, and boomerang communication are all defensive mechanisms."

Denial

Denial is a common defense. Imperative people just refuse to admit the truth—to others and sometimes even to themselves. They so strongly believe the lie that humanness is debilitating that they cannot bring themselves to admit even simple deficiencies.

Bob Wright frequently used denial to defend himself against Elaine's pleas to change some of his imperative behavior. For instance, when she mentioned how inconsistent Bob was in disciplining the boys, he responded, "You don't know what you're talking about." Or when she suggested that they should spend more time sharing personal needs with each other, he replied, "I give you more time than most men give their wives."

His flippant responses seemed to show his unwillingness to consider that she might have some worthwhile ideas. Yet Bob's defensive behavior was really motivated by fear. He was afraid of the changes he might have to make if he admitted that Elaine was right.

Evasiveness

Denial can often be an unconscious defense. The second type of defensive behavior, evasiveness, is premeditated. For several days before that explosive evening in the Wright household, Bob and Elaine had been bickering back and forth. That night Elaine had purposely decided, "If Bob wants to talk, he's going to have to find someone else to talk to. I'm going to ignore him." Although Elaine had reason to be frustrated, she only made matters worse by being evasive. Her fear of a confrontation was influencing her behavior. She had to be in control.

Boomerang Communication

We've all watched people play with boomerangs. A quick turn and that flying object comes back toward the person who threw it. Words can be turned around just as quickly—back toward the person who originally introduced the uncomfortable topic. For example, a father may bring attention to a son's messy bedroom only to hear the son reply, "Why don't you look at the junk piled on your desk if you want to talk about messes?"

No denial is attempted. Neither is the subject avoided. Instead the person protects himself or herself by becoming the aggressor.

Couples like Bob and Elaine often use boomerang communication. Watch Elaine send Bob's statement right back at him:

Bob: You're just too stubborn.
Elaine: If you want to talk about stubbornness, let's go over your behavior last Tuesday night. . . .

Since both of the Wrights used this defense, they might reverse the back-and-forth volley on another day. This time Bob sends Elaine's statement back to her:

Elaine: Oh, Bob, if you would just listen, really listen to me.
Bob: Do you ever listen to me when I have something to say?

Their verbal slings reveal their imperative thinking. Fear leads to defensiveness. You'll see how much the Wrights were missing if you compare this frustrating relationship with a healthy marriage in which two people share burdens, admit areas of need, and encourage each other.

For instance, the nondefensive person admits, "I'm not perfect. I have weaknesses and needs like everyone else, so I have no reason to pretend that I'm more important than you are." A healthy relationship admits that no person is ever "above it all." Honesty takes priority over pretenses.

How About You?

Do you use defensive behaviors to control others? Check the statements below that reflect your actions.

1. _____ "I work hard to create a friendly reputation so that I can keep others from seeing the other side of me."
2. _____ "If a topic is mentioned that is uncomfortable to me, I might leave the room or change the subject."
3. _____ "If someone exposes one of my weaknesses, I turn the tables and ask, 'What about you? You're just the same way.'"
4. _____ "I am perturbed when my opinions are not appreciated, and I wish I could get others to see my point of view."
5. _____ "I sometimes blame things that happen to me on other people. For instance, 'If you hadn't upset me so, I wouldn't have acted impatiently.'"
6. _____ "If I know someone is going to criticize me, I tend to be too busy to meet with him or her."

If you checked three of these statements, fear is causing you to be defensive. The imperative thought, "I've got to be above reproach," is driving your behavior.

As I talked to the Wrights, Elaine began to develop insight into the destructive effect of imperative thinking on their marriage.

"You know, I've noticed that my outward problems like anger and defensiveness aren't there when I'm feeling secure inside," Elaine reflected. "It's when I'm already tense from other things that I tend to take it out on Bob."

"What particular emotions seem to interfere with your communication with Bob?"

"Well," she said slowly, "I've always been a very conscientious person, which is good in a way. After all, it keeps me organized and sensitive to things that really matter. But it *does* cause me to become too easily worried. I get tense over things that shouldn't matter. And I scold myself too easily when something goes wrong."

I interjected, "So in addition to worry, you've been known to get caught in traps of guilt?"

"Yes, too easily. I want things right, and I'm my own worst critic. When I think something isn't done right, I become snappy and irritable."

"Have you always been so perfectionistic?"

"Yes. I was this way as early as my teen years. I remember feeling awful if I had facial blemishes or if I said something embarrassing at school. I never wanted to look foolish."

I knew we were making some real progress when Elaine was able to talk about her underlying emotions like this. Our emotions act in concert with one another, so Elaine could not overcome her defensive emotions (those that she directed at others) unless she also grappled with worry and guilt (emotions that are directed at ourselves). With that in mind, we spent time exploring the elements of her worry and guilt.

Worry

Worry can be defined as a feeling of apprehension, distress, or uneasiness, usually related to an anticipated event. Interestingly, our word *worry* originates from an Anglo-Saxon root word that means "to strangle or give pain." This implies that worry can literally paralyze us, sapping our energy and strength.

People who worry are not merely concerned about their present and future circumstances; they have a mental agenda of the way things *must* occur, much like that hypothetical contract of mine. The worrier's mind is so captivated by what *ought* or *ought not* to be, that he can only respond with duress and despair when situations displease him.

Four fallacies of imperative thinking make us susceptible to worry. The first is our tendency to focus on minutia.

Our Tendency to Focus on Minutia

Some decisions deserve a great deal of thought and subsequent follow-through. For instance, selecting the proper college for your teenager or the proper job for yourself. Many other subjects also deserve deliberation: the best ways to coordinate the schedules of family members or the proper furniture for your home. Such matters influence one's quality of life.

Many of the matters that consume our lives, however, fall into far less important categories. Daily we make trivial decisions, such as the color of socks to wear, the time to leave home for a social engagement, what to do about the dirty dishes, and so on. These minor decisions typically occupy a worrier's mind. In fact, these insignificant issues are often given much greater priority than the truly important ones.

Repeatedly, patients who are worriers insist that their anxiety is linked to a healthy concern for someone else's well-being. One of my patients meticulously cleaned his car each week so his family "could have the better things of life." Yet he was so compulsive about this activity that something else was obviously at stake. He was actually determined to satisfy his own need to be as perfect as possible.

If you're wondering if imperative thinking is causing you to worry needlessly, ask yourself the question, Who am I really concerned about? Myself or _____(my spouse, my children, my friend)?

The second fallacy that causes us to worry is our tendency to assume that the future will be a repeat of the past.

Our Tendency to Assume That the Future Will Repeat the Past

Many imperative people remember problems in the past and assume that the future will bring more of the same. These people vow, "I will never let this happen again." For example, a wife may recall the arguments, or perhaps physical abuse, from her childhood and vow, *We're not going to have such disagreements in our home.* She then expends tremendous energy trying to force harmony.

Worry about the repetition of past problems is not a sign of healthy thinking. True, it indicates a desire to be rid of the possibility of repeated pain, but invariably it represents its own brand of pain. The individual has clearly specified what must—and what must not—be part of his life, but the mind is so obsessed with preventing old problems that satisfaction is not recognized in present situations. The imperative person is a prisoner of the past.

Another fallacy that causes excessive worry is our tendency to assume the worst.

Our Tendency to Assume the Worst

Even when everything is going well, the worrier assumes, "It's only a matter of time before something will go wrong." Worriers think, *I'm trying to preserve the good in my life.* Unfortunately they are so consumed with trying to eliminate potential problems that the slightest problems are seen as potential disasters. Though most are not willing to admit it, they create the very tension they want to avoid.

Elaine once complained to Bob, "Why do you have to be so uptight when you're doing things with me and the boys? You're so ready to pounce on the boys or me if we say the wrong thing or do something that doesn't fit into your agenda."

Somewhat defensively Bob replied, "Well, maybe I wouldn't be so worried if I knew that you used more common sense. Some of the things you allow the boys to do are unreasonable. Do you expect me just to sit quietly and smile during those situations?"

"Oh, come on," Elaine objected. "You know the boys are well mannered, and each of them knows what he can and cannot do."

"Bob, it seems that Elaine feels that you too often assume the worst," I interjected. "What do you think?"

"I wouldn't say I assume the worst. It's just that I like to know that we're not going to have catastrophes. Say whatever you will, but I want to be sure that my family has positive memories, not negative ones."

Bob's unbending attitudes caused him to react too strongly to the things he did not like. He then became unable to see the good in his life.

The final fallacy that causes us to worry needlessly is our tendency to lack confidence in ourselves.

Our Tendency to Lack Confidence in Ourselves

Perhaps the element that causes worry to be a never-ending trait is an underlying lack of self-confidence.

Bob Wright tended to fret over minor matters, like slight conflicts in his and Elaine's schedules. One Saturday he got upset with Elaine because he thought her activities might interfere with his weekly tennis match with a friend when, in fact, she had accommodated her schedule to his tennis game. As he told me about the tension he had experienced, I asked, "Can you see how you are actually giving yourself a vote of no confidence?"

"What do you mean?" he queried. "I'm confident enough, most of the time."

"While you don't actually say it, your worry communicates: 'I have serious doubts about my ability to handle less-than-perfect behavior in my wife.' You're presuming you would fall apart if your specifications were not met."

Bob shifted his position in the chair and looked at me incredulously, "Well, if that's what I was thinking I sure wasn't aware of it."

Yet that's exactly what he was thinking. Bob felt he had to iron out all the problems in his world in order to be okay.

How About You?

Is your imperative thinking causing you to worry unduly? Check the statements below that apply to you to find out:

1. ____ "I tend to assume the worst when a problem arises."
2. ____ "I must have my activities planned well in advance, so little can go wrong at the last minute."

3. ____ "When I have to do something new or different, I sometimes feel anxious or tense or I get a
headache."
4. ____ "I'd rather live within predictable guidelines
than try new ways."
5. ____ "I always insist on exactness, even when such
precision is not necessary."
6. ____ "Cleanliness and order are very important to
me. I'm uneasy if everything isn't just right."
7. ____ "When someone in my family makes a mistake, I quickly come up with an excuse or apol-
ogy."

If you checked three or more statements, imperative
thinking is causing you to worry unduly. The other internal emotion that is frequently driven by imperative
thinking is guilt.

Guilt

No person can ever be perfect, so a natural by-
product of imperative thinking is false guilt, one of the
most destructive emotions. Imperative people are prone
to guilt. Their inner standards can be so impossible that
they can try and try to appease their consciences when
wrongdoing occurs, but an inner voice always commands them to do more.

True guilt promotes responsible living and nudges us
toward healthy accountability; it creates a powerful discomfort that keeps us from resting easily until we rectify
the wrong. Then we can accept forgiveness from God
and from the ones wronged. A healthy response to guilt
requires an acceptance of ourselves, imperfections and
all. But imperative people have difficulty with a concept
like acceptance. They try to fit life into a concrete,
black-or-white mold, which often says you perform
properly or else.

Guilt played a major role in Elaine and Bob Wright's problems. Each one of them was a pro at inducing false guilt in the other, and each one of them was susceptible to carrying that false guilt.

For example, Bob told me of an incident when he had been too harsh with John, his younger son. He had mistakenly assumed that John had joined some friends in a sports outing when, in fact, Bob had never told John he could go. After Bob punished John (who, of course, acted very confused at his dad's behavior), Elaine made Bob think back over that day, which caused him to realize that he had never told John he *couldn't* go either. Elaine reminded Bob, "This has happened before. You frequently make punitive decisions without really thinking about what happened."

At our next counseling session Bob told me about the incident. "Elaine's right," he admitted. "I do get overzealous in my punishment of the boys. I mean well, but I foul up too easily. Sometimes I think they'd be better off if I wasn't around."

"Now wait a minute, Bob," I urged. "You're not perfect; nobody is, but now you're tending to condemn yourself too strongly. You have very high personal standards and you get disgusted when you fall short."

"My problem," said Bob, "is that I fall short too often. I don't know . . . maybe I'm just not the family man I'm supposed to be."

Some of Bob's guilt was healthy; he was capable of making errors, sometimes serious ones, so he needed an internal guidance system to get him back on track. Bob's problem was that he took on too much blame. Rather than responding to his mistakes with normal repentance, he heaped condemnation on himself. This was caused by the imperative thought, "I *must* be a perfect father."

The telltale indicators of how imperative thinking twists guilt are abundant. Check the statements below that apply to your own feelings of guilt:

1. ___ "I feel that I need to make up for my mistakes by proving how good I really am."
2. ___ "I tend to make too many excuses for my mistakes and imperfections."
3. ___ "When I compare myself to other people, I tend to assume that they are better than I am."
4. ___ "I am easily intimidated by another person's strong attitudes, even though I know that person is wrong."
5. ___ "Even though people tell me they've forgiven me, I never really feel forgiven."
6. ___ "I apologize more than I need to."

If you checked three or more of these statements, imperative thinking has you in its grip.

The Lies Behind Imperative Thinking

To help Bob Wright, and the many others like him who are so susceptible to false guilt, I expose the lies that undergird imperative thinking:

- "I must make perfect restitution."
- "Other people's opinions are all-important."

I Must Make Perfect Restitution

Imperative people demand so much of themselves that they never feel they can make up for their mistakes. Instead they view their acts of restitution as a *requirement,* which *might or might not* absolve their guilt.

For example, Elaine recalled a time when she accidentally forgot to invite an acquaintance to a bridal shower she was hosting. Once she became aware of this social mistake, she felt terribly guilty. She was tormented with thoughts like *How could I have made such a blunder?* and *I'm embarrassed to have to face my friend again.* Her imperative agenda did not allow her to make an error.

I asked her, "Wouldn't it be enough to admit your mistake to your friend, then determine to triple check the guest list the next time you host a shower?"

Her response revealed her unbending mindset. "But that wouldn't erase what has been done. Now every time I see this woman I'll feel very awkward. I can't believe I let myself make such a simple mistake."

Imperative people can work through guilt if they realize that no human being is capable of undoing wrongs (We aren't God!) and reject this impossible standard.

Other People's Opinions Are All-Important

Some imperative persons are *too* desirous of receiving input from others. Painfully aware of our inability to live perfectly, we think, "Maybe others can give me instructions that will help me stay in control." We literally become slaves to public opinion.

Elaine reminisced, "I remember as a girl how easily I was controlled by guilt. My dad could just give me *the look* and I would cry. I would do anything to keep him happy."

Bob nodded his head in agreement. "If a friend is upset with her, Elaine's in a stew, even when she hasn't done anything wrong."

"Let's analyze what's making you feel that way, Elaine," I suggested. "Your guilt is fed by the imperative thought that you must appease others. As you do this, you give others a godlike power over you."

"I know you're right," Elaine said sheepishly. "I want to believe that other people's opinions are not infallible."

Elaine needed to see other people's opinions as just as fallible as her own. No human being is God.

The Inevitable Result: Interpersonal Turmoil

When imperative thinking directs our emotions, it becomes impossible to maintain our composure. We lose our temper. Then we feel guilty and we worry about our relationship with others. This negative cycle continually perpetuates itself.

That's why I help my patients to understand how their backgrounds and their human nature have contributed to their actions. In Part Two I will ask you to answer four questions:

- Are you driven by duty?
- Are you unconsciously dependent upon other people's opinions and emotions?
- Do you act superior, yet feel inferior?
- Do you have an inborn craving for control?

As you identify with these traits of an imperative personality, I will help you to understand how your background and your human nature have contributed to these actions—and how you can free yourself from the need to always be in control.

PART TWO

Understanding the Pieces of an Imperative Personality

CHAPTER 4

Are You Driven by Duty?

Slightly overweight, in her late thirties, Carol Browning had the casual "down home" appearance of someone you could trust. It was clear as she spoke with me that she would be the type of person others could place confidence in.

"I'm really embarrassed that I'm in your counseling office trying to make sense of my emotions," she said. "I mean, all my life I've been careful to do what is right. I've established a reputation of reliability. In fact, when my friends have problems, *I'm* the one they call because they can always count on me to help them. Now here I am, asking for help. It makes no sense to me that I can't get a handle on myself."

As Carol told me about the events in her recent past, I quickly understood why she was experiencing tension. Her marriage had always been satisfactory. Better, in fact, than most. But lately she felt pushed out of her husband's world. He had been laid off from work a year earlier and was now adjusting to a new position with a new company. His hours were longer, and even when he was at home, his mind seemed to be somewhere else. This bothered Carol, but she wasn't the type to complain openly. Additionally, her father had recently died, and her mother had been placed in a nursing home because of a degenerative bone condition. The oldest of three daughters and the only one near their mother, Carol had the responsibility of seeing to her many needs. Although the nursing home was the only real option, Carol felt guilty about putting her there, and this guilt ate away at her self-esteem. Add this to the fact that her two grade-school children were quite busy in school and sports activities, and it was no wonder Carol felt overwhelmed, as if the weight of all the family's burdens rested on her shoulders.

"My friends keep telling me I ought to cut back on my responsibilities, but I don't see how I can!" she insisted. "Everyone is counting on me. If I just decide to take a day off, a lot of people will be left holding the bag. Unfortunately, I have no other option but to press on."

Despite her tension, Carol smiled easily, and I could tell that she possessed the kind of common sense that enabled her to help unravel the personal struggles of other people. To know Carol was to like her. Playing a hunch I said, "You've mentioned some of your current family obligations, but I suspect you also busy yourself with other responsibilities. What else are you involved in?"

"I've always felt I should give time to the community, especially where it concerns my children. So I'm a homeroom mother in both of my kids' classes. That keeps me hopping with several activities per month. Also, I teach one of the children's choirs each week at church. I like it, but it's sometimes frustrating because the other directors don't always seem as willing to do their share. Also, every Tuesday and Thursday I take a class in home decorating." She laughed a little self-consciously. "Well, my friends are always calling me for decorating advice, so I thought I might as well get some formal training," she explained.

"From the sound of it, you hardly ever slow down."

"Too busy!" she responded. "Maybe I'm experiencing burnout. The thing is, I'm feeling less and less inclined to want to help people. I've never been an angry person, but I sure have been irritable lately. Sometimes I sit down and try to figure out how I can trim my schedule, but I always start feeling guilty if I leave someone out."

"Carol, I suspect this pattern is nothing new. How far back do you remember being so responsible?"

She smiled. "Oh, that's easy. Mother tells me that before I was in the first grade, I was helping take care of my younger sister. And as I grew older, she really relied on me a lot to be the baby sitter. I helped with meals and cleaning too. I was real handy to have around!"

"And I assume you continued this habit at school too?"

"Well, sure! I made good grades and was always the teacher's pet. I never lacked friends or things to do because I was usually the one planning everything."

"So your lifestyle now is really not very different from what you've known for years, but you've finally reached a point of overload."

Carol nodded. Then she said, "You know, I've always had this fear of not doing something just right. I suppose I put more effort into things than I need to, but I'm afraid I won't be successful without that extra effort." She sighed. "You can't imagine how relieved I am when I've done a good job." Then she leaned forward, and her voice was serious. "Dr. Carter, I feel like I may be sliding into some sort of depression, and that's just not me. I've got to get to the root of this because I can't afford to have any down time."

The Dutiful Mindset

As I listened to Carol's list of activities, it became clear that she had too much of a good thing. That is, while I certainly applauded her desire to serve and to be trustworthy, I sensed that she was putting so much pressure on herself to perform that her feeling of depression was an inevitable result. No one could sustain the impossible expectations she had placed on herself.

This same mindset exists in the vast majority of the imperative people I have counseled. Not all are as self-conscious and driven as Carol, but most have placed far too much emphasis on achievement and conformity throughout their lives.

Strange as it may sound, imperative people can have too strong a sense of responsibility. In pushing themselves to *do right,* they often pay the price of burnout. When others encourage them to slow down, they won't for fear that a bad habit of laziness might develop. Or perhaps someone will be displeased. The saying "When you want something done, ask the busiest person in town to do it" may contain a lot of truth. Especially if the busiest person in town doesn't have the ability to say no.

How About You?

Certainly I encourage individuals to know their responsibilities. But maintaining a balance and living within healthy guidelines will help us remain emotionally stable. If you see your responsibility to others as a duty rather than an option, your privilege of choice has given way to sheer obligation. Stop for a moment to analyze your motives by checking the statements below that apply to you:

1. ____ "I do kind things for other people to repay them for their kindness to me."
2. ____ "I say yes to a request only because I feel others would be disappointed in me if I said no."
3. ____ "After a task is completed, I look forward to an evaluation of my work as my payoff."
4. ____ "I smile when I am not really happy, just to please others."
5. ____ "I seldom confront other people for fear of offending them, yet on occasion when I'm really upset I may swing the other way and be too aggressive."
6. ____ "It is very important that I maintain an unblemished reputation."

If you checked three of the above statements, you tend to emphasize duty over choice.

In many cases, duty-driven people are highly regarded since they have a reputation for reliability and friendliness. They often seem to be perfectly happy with all their activities; yet when a person is too motivated by duty, that person is living a lie. Eventually he feels trapped, frustrated, distraught, burned out.

Environmental Factors of Dutiful Living

What causes some of us to be people pleasers? Imperative people often develop this tendency in their childhood years, then continue throughout adulthood. The following common experiences lead to an excessive sense of duty.

1. *The Outer Self Gets Top Billing*

During your early years your parents undoubtedly tried to teach you responsible behavior. They said,

"Don't talk back to grownups," and "Close your mouth when you chew your food." Teachers said, "Put your name in the upper right hand corner of your paper," and "Raise your hand before you speak." Parents assigned chores (perhaps with elaborate charts posted on the refrigerator door where no one could miss them), and you soon learned to expect certain consequences if each responsibility was not accomplished.

Think about your childhood experiences. Did your parents spend a lot of time teaching you the outward behavior that would make you a responsible adult? I don't mean to imply that there's anything wrong with this if it's not carried too far, but did you ever have an opportunity to talk about the way you *felt?* Were you able to admit you were angry or irritable or afraid? Did anyone take time to help you understand why you felt these kinds of emotions? Children who don't have this kind of encouragement gradually learn to suppress their negative feelings. It is easier to pretend that you don't have them than to be criticized for expressing them.

For example, Carol recalled many childhood incidences of friction with her younger sisters. Typically her mother would intervene with a statement like, "Young lady, you're going to have to stop arguing with Helen. If you don't quit, you can't use the phone this evening."

On the surface, Carol's mother's response would seem to be proper, and it did usually produce the desired results. But notice the focus. No discussion was ever given to Carol's emotions. She was merely told *what to do*. The message was clear: *How you feel is of little importance around here.*

Instead Carol needed someone to say, "Let's talk about why you're feeling so upset," and "Let's think about ways you can be more composed." Without this training Carol learned to respond to irritating situations in the only way she knew: "Do what is right because you have to." She never thought about why she was feeling the way she was.

2. *Emotions Are Graded: A, B, or C*

When children enter school, they immediately become aware of the importance of grades. Each effort at reading, writing, and arithmetic is closely scrutinized and an evaluation follows. Grades communicate how successfully a child is accomplishing the requirements, so (rightly or wrongly) they quickly become the basis for a child's self-esteem. Additionally, grades become a source of comparison and competition. Children are very sensitive to the pecking order in the classroom. They quickly learn which students are the top achievers and which are the "ne'er do well's." Too often, making a good grade becomes more important than learning.

But school is not the only place where we are graded. At home, at church, and even among peers, children receive grades for a wide variety of matters. For example, children know that their parents will evaluate how well a bedroom is cleaned. They might hear, "You've done an excellent job," or perhaps, "You're going to have to do better than this," or even, "Get back in there and don't come out until it's *clean!*" Children are often motivated by such phrases as "Michael doesn't argue when his mother tells him what to do. Why can't you be more like Michael?" Or a parent might examine a school project and comment, "This looks okay, but I know you can do better if you try."

Grading is even common when a child expresses an emotion. Sometimes the grade is clearly spoken in a phrase like, "I like you a lot better when you're pleasant and not grumpy." Other times it is implied in a statement like, "I don't know what's gotten into you, but you'd better get that look off your face." Children learn early in life that if they are going to get along with others, they need to maximize the good emotions and hide the bad ones. Permission to be genuine is not allowed. Black-and-white thinking—"You should not do this. You must do that!"—directs the child's life.

Carol admitted in one of our sessions, "I think I have problems with my emotions now because I never really learned how to talk about them with someone who could help me understand my ups and downs."

"Let me guess," I offered. "When you felt angry, perhaps bitter, you assumed that you'd better keep it to yourself because you might get in trouble if you exposed a feeling that didn't match your reputation as a nice, well-behaved girl."

"Oh, absolutely. I couldn't dare admit to having a negative feeling—let alone allow it to come out in the open. My parents would have thought I was horrible if I had ever let on that I felt so strongly about something."

Probing her to explore the implication of this pattern I asked, "Did your negative feelings just disappear and go away after a while?"

"I guess not. In fact, I know they didn't because I can remember many times when I was so angry about something that I mulled it over and over in my mind until it seemed to be all I could think about. If anything, I guess my feelings grew stronger. I didn't know what to do with them, so I finally just sort of swallowed them." She began to laugh. "It's a wonder I don't have chronic indigestion."

Instead of having to cover up unsettling emotions—or "swallow" them, as Carol did—children need permission to explore their feelings. By no means does this imply that a "let 'er rip" philosophy should prevail in the home. Boundaries and consequences are necessary parts of parent-child communication. But it does mean that labeling a child as good or bad, based on emotional expressions, *can* eventually lead to an imperative style of living.

Emotions, pleasant and unpleasant, are a natural part of what we are. Therefore, each person needs to examine their meaning in order to make healthy emotional responses. Carol wasn't able to do this as a child. Now, as an adult, she needed to take time to examine her emotions. I encouraged her to ask herself:

- "Why am I feeling this way?"
- "What are my choices?"
- "What behavior will ease the tension?"

I pointed out that Carol might need to ask a whole series of "why" questions, having an extended conversation with herself, before she got to the root of a troublesome emotion.

At our next appointment, Carol laughed. "Les, when I asked myself those questions, I began to feel like I was on a quiz show."

"Why not start at the beginning and tell me all about it."

"Well, it all started when I agreed to teach a Sunday school class. It was a dumb thing to do, with all the other commitments I have."

"Why did you agree?"

"Wait a minute, Les. Those are my lines, remember? As soon as I realized I was feeling depressed, I did exactly what you told me. I sat down and had a conversation with myself. It went something like this:

'Why are you depressed, Carol?'
'Because I'm tired.'

'Why are you tired?'
'Because I have too much to do.'
'Why do you have too much to do?'
'Because I keep saying *yes* to people.'
'Why do you do that?'
'Because I don't have good sense.'
'That's not an honest answer, Carol. Let's try again.'
'Okay. I keep saying yes because people expect it.'
'Do you always do what people expect you to do?'
'I guess I do . . . anyway, most of the time.'
'Why is that?'
'Because people won't like me otherwise.'
'Do people only like you because of the things you do?'

"That was a horrible thought, Les. But I suddenly understood all the backlog of misdirected thinking that was behind my depression. Then I remembered to ask myself what I could do about this, and I realized I had several choices.

- I could teach and still be depressed about it.
- I could teach and give up the children's choir, which I really enjoy.
- I could find someone to teach in my place.
- I could explain that I have enough to do and really don't want to take on any more responsibilities.

"I knew that only one of these choices was the right one. I went straight to the telephone and called the church. You know, when I explained why I didn't want the job, people were really understanding. And I felt great for handling a problem honestly."

By asking herself why she was feeling depressed, by considering her choices, and by deciding on behavior that would ease her tension, Carol was able to better understand her own feelings, realize why she had responded to circumstances by trying to be all things to all people, and move toward healthier responses in the future.

3. *Personal Value Is Earned*

When I talk with imperative people like Carol, I often hear the word *but* when they describe the atmosphere of love in their early family life.

- "I know my parents loved me, *but* I couldn't dare let them know when I got in trouble at school."
- "My dad was friendly in public, *but* he could fly into a tirade if we ever got out of line at home."
- "Mom would do anything in the world for us, *but* I knew better than to mention certain sensitive subjects."

I'm sure you heard the same clues I did. Carol couldn't dare let her parents know when she got in trouble at school; her dad flew into a tirade if she got out of line at home; her mom would not let her mention certain subjects. No amount of transgression was permitted. Carol must be perfect. She was insecure about her true value because she knew she could never perform as perfectly as Mom and Dad expected. As an adult, the unconscious tapes in her mind replayed her parents' standards every time she made a mistake. Carol often asked, "Why should I be so anxious that my friends not find out about my mistakes?"

"You are sure hard on yourself," I responded. "First you scold yourself for having weaknesses, then you pour more salt into the wound by demanding that you be superhuman."

When the message "It's not how you perform that makes me love you; I love you simply because you are you" is not a part of our early years, we often spend the rest of our lives trying to be good enough to be loved, a futile quest. Persons like Carol can ease their tense emotions only when they develop a freer foundation of thought: "My worth as a human is God-given and not tied to my latest performance."

People like Carol may have heard all their lives that the personal worth of individuals is simply part of being human. Perhaps they learned this in their early years in Sunday school, or maybe they have even instructed their own children to love others because God loves all people. Yet in reality the idea of innate value seems too abstract. The obligation to perform correctly caused them to judge themselves so strictly when errors occurred that worth became a prize to be sought, not a given fact.

4. *Thinking About Options Is Not Encouraged*

A former Marine told me that he was not expected to think about the options in a given situation. He was expected to do whatever his instructor told him, without question. So it is in the development of imperative living. There may not necessarily have been a Marine-like atmosphere in Carol's home; nevertheless, options were not freely discussed when personal or emotional issues arose.

In one session, Carol told me about a recent argument she had with her eleven-year-old daughter, Lana. She had been particularly frustrated by the breakdown in their communication because it had been so reminiscent of similar scenes when she was a girl.

"Lana was invited to go to a party at a friend's house, and I learned there would be some boys there," she told me. "It bothered me because all her friends are in a boy-crazy phase, and I wasn't sure they would behave. So I

told her she should not get carried away if some of the
kids wanted to play kissing games. She became furious
that I would even suggest such a thing. I think she was
just embarrassed, but the more I tried to explain my
point of view, the angrier she got. She acted like I didn't
trust her, and I ended up feeling like I must have a dirty
mind. It turned into a pretty ugly scene."

"Carol, you mentioned earlier that this was similar to
some episodes between you and your mother. Tell me
about them."

"Oh, it played out in almost exactly the same way. In
fact, I was probably using the very reasoning my
mother used when she lectured me!"

Parents and teachers often have such very strong
convictions that they feel they must pass them along to
children—convictions made stronger by the fact that
they have a powerful emotional investment in the child.
So often they end up speaking zealously and uttering
all-or-nothing commands.

Think back to your own childhood. Did your parents
speak in a way that allowed you to feel you were participating in setting limits? Did you ever discuss moral values and feel that you were being encouraged to make
responsible decisions? Were you allowed to express
your point of view?

I'm not implying that a parent should never set firm
boundaries for children. That might lead to chaos. But
time can be spent discussing the why's of behavior and
listening to each other's opinions.

I recall one woman who protested the idea of discussing options with her children. "My kids would run absolutely wild if I gave them choices," she said. "If I don't
stay right on top of them, they'll never learn to live correctly."

Respecting her desire for orderliness, but questioning her dictatorial manner, I responded, "I'm thinking more of your children's future when Mom won't be around to tell them what to do. They'll have so little practice in making healthy decisions that chaos will almost be guaranteed."

Maintaining control is an ever-present goal of the imperative person. Conversely, relinquishing control and encouraging another person to think and reason are the goals of healthy interpersonal relations.

As I talked to Carol, I could see that she was both excited and apprehensive about the idea of having options. Making choices was not yet a natural experience for her.

"I've always wished people would give me the opportunity to think for myself," she confided.

"Carol, you don't need to wait for someone to give you permission to think," I told her. "You can start considering your options right now."

When she looked a little doubtful, I assured her that she didn't have to start out by changing the world. "You can begin with simple things," I urged. For example:

- When someone asks you to serve on a committee, say to yourself, "I can accept or refuse; it's up to me."
- When your husband says you should do something, ask yourself this question: "Is it important enough to do today, or can I put it off until tomorrow?"

While these were not earth-shaking alternatives, they did provide a different experience for Carol—a chance for her to give herself permission to make her own choices.

5. *Religion and Morality Are Dogmatic but Shallow*

Most adults can recall moments in childhood when they were given instruction about how a good Christian or a respectable person should behave. Too commonly, these discussions ended before you or I had a chance to understand the reasoning behind our parents' or teachers' words. Most kids just learn: Christians *can* do this; they'd *better not* do that. As adults, our religious and moral ethics are firm, but shallow. We have never thought about why we believe what we believe.

Carol seemed to feel guilty as she told me, "Lately I've been a lot less interested in my spiritual life. This feels strange to me since I've always been considered the pious one in the family. In fact, I've been the family's conscience on many occasions, and I've held my husband and kids to very high standards."

"What would happen if you questioned some of your own values?" I asked.

"There wouldn't be any point in trying. I've always known that the Christian way of life was the only way. I've accepted the rules as something I had to do. It's too late to question them now."

Dogmatic morality may produce the correct external results for a while. But when Carol finally grappled for a *reason* to live out her Christian beliefs, she became depressed by the struggle. Yet if she had decided to rebel, as other people have, she would have been haunted by guilt and worry.

Carol needed time out to meditate and contemplate. *Why* should she continue to pursue the morality that had always guided her? Pat answers wouldn't do. She needed the opportunity to think through hard questions like:

- Why would I want to be a servant?
- Is pleasantness always the best trait to project?
- What is my responsibility in setting limits?
- How is that part of the healthy Christian life?

6. *Unique Perceptions Are Disallowed*

During one of our sessions I brought up the subject of disagreement. "Carol," I said, "I'm sure you've experienced many different occasions when you didn't see eye to eye with other people. But I'm curious. How free have you been to air those differences?"

"Oh, not at all," she replied. "I never felt I could afford to be viewed as a contrary person."

"Why is that?"

"Well, when I was young my family put a premium on being cooperative. We all had chores to do, and we had to perform them with no complaints. In public we knew that we were expected to set a good example, and that meant we couldn't be rowdy or disrespectful. If my parents taught me one thing well it was *Don't create a disturbance.*"

"Carol, I think you know me well enough to know that I certainly appreciate a cooperative spirit. But I can't help wondering if you learned these things *too* well."

"I know that I've always been careful to filter my words and actions through other people's eyes," she said. "It makes me uncomfortable to feel like I'm being controversial—or even just different." She was silent for a minute. "You know, this problem exists right now in my marriage. My husband is a wonderful and helpful man, but he does *not* like me to disagree with him or to get angry with our kids."

"Strangely enough, Carol, when you keep yourself from expressing a different opinion, you actually increase the tension between you and another person—just what you're trying to avoid. The fact is, you're not being honest with yourself or with others."

While Carol did not need to go overboard in expressing herself, she did need to realize that she could express her own point of view.

Carol needed to tell herself every day:

- "It's okay for me to say no!"
- "I don't have to shoulder the blame whenever someone has hurt feelings."
- "It's okay to stand up for my convictions, even if others don't agree."
- "It's okay for me to be different."
- "It's okay for other people to be different."
- "It's okay to take time for myself, to relax and enjoy life."
- "My personal worth is not earned; it is God-given."

CHAPTER 5

Are You Dependent?

A former college football player now in his late thirties, Jack was an imposing figure whose rock-solid frame commanded immediate attention when he entered a room. It was easy to picture him twenty years younger cajoling and horsing around with the guys in the locker room. Pleasantly outgoing and always ready with a witty story, Jack was now a natural salesman. He put his skills to good use year after year as he led his insurance company in new business advancements.

Jack had come to my counseling office at the insistence of his wife, Claire. In an earlier phone conversation, she had told me that he was virtually impossible to live with. Whenever she or one of their three children displeased him, he commanded them to do as he ordered. He required a weekly accounting of his wife's spending. If she spent more money than he thought she should or bought something he thought was frivolous, he deducted that amount from her next week's allowance. If she cried or expressed fear or worry, Jack told her to "straighten up."

After years of living in fear of his criticisms, Claire had issued an ultimatum: "Either you get counseling or I'll divorce you." That's why Jack was here, sitting reluctantly in the chair opposite me.

"Jack, I'm always interested to know what brings people to my office. I understand there have been tensions in your home, but I want to hear your side of the story. Why don't you describe the circumstances as you see them."

"Well, I know you've already talked to Claire, and I'm sure she's told you how much trouble we've had lately. Even though she may not feel that I love her, I think I'm a pretty lucky husband. She really tries hard. The problems is more with me, I guess. I've got a temper that can sometimes get nasty. I know Claire and the kids get frustrated with me, but to tell you the truth, *I'm* just as frustrated with me."

It was refreshing to hear Jack take responsibility like this; imperative people often tend to push all their problems off on someone else. Wanting to hear more about his emotional patterns, I asked, "What sorts of things make you irritable?"

"It's really kinda hard to say," he replied. "I mean, I usually get out of sorts with small things. For instance, it bugs me when my wife wastes money. It's not as if we're on the edge of bankruptcy, but I hate to see our money wasted on trivial items. And the kids have annoying habits like squabbling with each other or talking back when I tell them what to do. It can go on for only so long; then I let them know exactly how I feel. Of course, you don't need me to tell you that this only makes matters worse."

"Jack, I'm impressed with the fact that you're willing to examine your emotions. Can you tell me how you feel about being in control?"

"Maybe you'll believe me, maybe you won't. I really don't get any great thrill out of it. But I just can't stand disorder! Something inside me cringes every time Claire speaks in a whiny tone or every time my children show disrespect. It's like a switch goes off in my mind and I have to say something. I have to take over. If I keep quiet, I feel tense inside. Sometimes I really feel like I'm ready to explode."

I prodded Jack to do some more exploring. "Jack, it's clear that your emotional stability hinges on the behavior of the people around you. That's not a very solid foundation for real stability."

"Are you saying I'm an insecure person?" he asked.

"I guess you could draw that conclusion," I said. "Jack, your need to be in control is an indicator that you only feel composed if your world treats you right. When something gets out of line—and it inevitably does—your mood quickly goes sour. You are signing a 100 percent guarantee of emotional problems because your world will never give you precisely what you think you want or need."

"But don't we all do what you just suggested?" he asked. "Isn't everybody's mood controlled by the people and events around them?"

"That's true to some extent," I admitted. "But that doesn't mean it's a healthy habit. I'm noticing that you're exhibiting the trait of dependency—your feelings are too easily guided by others' emotions or behaviors. You're responding by trying to get control, but it's not working. It's possible to learn a delicate detachment from others so we won't in turn feel the need to control their behavior."

Recognizing Dependency

We often think of dependency as a trait of persons
with weak egos who chronically defer to others' opinions and preferences. Presumably, dependent persons
appear insecure, incapable to making decisions, easily
dominated. So we assume that if someone is strong-
willed, decisive, or controlling, that person cannot possibly be dependent.

There *is* a psychological profile called the dependent
personality type, which is too easily dominated. But dependency is a much broader trait than the stereotype
would suggest. In fact, it is present to some degree in
every personality. Surprisingly, imperative people are
often quite emotionally dependent.

Many imperative people will balk at being described
as dependent. (Jack had certainly never thought of himself that way.) Pointing to their organizational skills or
their strong opinions, they will claim to be highly self-
sufficient. Close examination shows that independence
in tasks does not always translate into emotional independence. Being performers, imperative people instinc-
tively watch for other people's reactions, and they
experience strong emotions when others do not respond as expected.

To see if dependency is playing a role in your imperative tendencies, check the following statements that relate to yourself.

_____ "After I give my opinion, I tend to press my point
of view again if the listener is not in agreement
with me."

_____ "When I see an associate or family member acting in a way that bothers me, I get antsy and want
to correct his or her ways."

_____ "It is difficult for me to listen quietly when someone is expressing an opinion I disagree with."

_____ "I maintain my composure when my day unfolds as planned, but glitches in my schedule create real uneasiness."

_____ "I don't always reveal my full feelings or preferences when I think others are likely to frown on my thoughts."

_____ "When someone gives me a rebuttal, I give a counter rebuttal."

_____ "I am known to question others openly when their decisions disagree with mine."

_____ "I deliberately avoid people who are as strong willed as I am."

If you checked four or more of these statements, your inner peace, like Jack's, is too contingent on other people's behavior.

Patterns that Feed Excessive Dependency

In the ensuing sessions, Jack and I discussed how his imperative lifestyle could be altered so he could be less dependent.

At one point he shook his head and said to me, "No one has ever called me dependent before. I used to think only women and weaklings were dependent."

Despite his aversion to the term, we decided together that it was healthy to call dependency by its name. We concluded that while it was not entirely wrong for his moods to be influenced by others, he could relate more successfully with his family as he became aware of this trait's excesses. This change required insights into several learned patterns.

1. *Other People Are Responsible for the Way I Feel*

I explained to Jack that when there has not been a steady opportunity for a child to identify and explore his problems, he will be too dependent upon other people's responses when he becomes an adult.

"Jack, each young child has a natural inclination toward dependency. I didn't know you when you were a boy, yet I'm sure you must have looked toward your parents or teachers or coaches whenever a difficulty surfaced. You wondered about the way they expected you to handle yourself."

Jack nodded. "I'd always try to act like I thought the adults wanted me to act. If I had strong contrary feelings, I just kept them to myself. I used to think I'd get in trouble if I admitted to feeling scared or hateful or resentful."

"Let's see what this taught you," I said. "You learned to say to yourself: 'I can't afford to think for myself about how I can resolve my problems. That's too dangerous. I can only do what they want me to do.' Your actions, then, were not a matter of inner decision making; instead they filtered through your assumptions about other people's reactions."

"But, Les, I'm not so sure I would have handled my problems correctly even if I had felt able to make all my own choices."

"I imagine you're right. Kids don't begin life with the best insights for healthy living. I'm suggesting that children need constant encouragement and instruction about how to draw the best choices from within themselves. This involves a certain amount of freedom and the expectation that there will be trial and error."

"And that's where I get frustrated now," Jack admitted, "especially when there's error."

"Think of it this way, Jack. If I take my car to the local automotive shop for mechanical repairs and the mechanic goofs up on the job, I feel I must tell him to do a better job of repairing my car. Similarly, the person with strong imperative tendencies insists that others should repair his troublesome situations. When those people err, imperative people use coercion. This behavior may appear to be the most glaring problem, but it's driven by dependency."

2. *I'm Not the Person I Want to Be*

In my years of counseling I have found that most people know how they should relate to others. Very early in life someone told each of us to share, to forgive, to follow the Golden Rule. Being apprised of the *facts* of good living is rarely a problem.

Problems abound for many, though, when it is time to apply those facts. Imperative people, in particular, have a hard time translating this knowledge into daily living. I don't mean that we *never* exhibit such traits because we often do. Rather, we frustrate ourselves by our inconsistencies. As one woman put it, "I don't need anyone to tell me that I ought to be patient with my children, loving toward my husband, and devoted in my spiritual life, but how can I when the kids are so unruly, my husband so inattentive, and my church life such a bore?"

When imperative people are challenged with distasteful circumstances, the good knowledge is set aside. In the end, we are held captive by our surroundings. Externals rather than internals guide our emotions and direct our behavior.

This was certainly true with Jack. He told me, "I see other men with their children, and I feel envious because they seem to have it together. They are everything I'm not. They are patient while I'm set off by little things that shouldn't matter. They are encouraging while I'm critical. Their kids like being with them, but mine seem fine without me."

"I'm assuming, Jack, that you have some notions about how you'd like to be, but somehow your plans falter when your kids don't seem to respect you."

"You said that right." He shook his head. "I may not read many books like you do, but I do know what kind of dad I'd like to be. Something just isn't working out the way I'd like."

Prodding him, I suggested, "It would be helpful if you could learn to anticipate disruptive situations, then make very specific plans as to how you will respond. For example, as you go home each evening, you can tell yourself that patience will guide you during the first hour with your family. In advance, you can refuse to get pulled into their tensions."

"But what happens if things start to get out of control, despite all my good intentions? How do I stop myself from taking control when I'm in the center of the situation?"

"That's a good question, Jack, because it shows that you're aware of those times when you're likely to get into trouble. These are the times when you need to practice that "delicate detachment" that we talked about earlier. This means having a little objectivity, placing yourself outside the situation and looking in."

I explained to Jack that "delicate detachment" doesn't mean not caring. It just means distancing yourself far enough from the firing line so that you can think straight again. I suggested some practical things he might do to implement this kind of objectivity:

- Walk out of the room. This removes you physically from the turmoil and is an instant way to keep you from reaching out and trying to "fix things" your way.
- Take a few deep breaths. Slow yourself down so your temper has a chance to cool off.
- Get your thoughts in order. Think about your choices in the particular situation that is facing you.
- Say a prayer. Ask God to take control, and then *give* Him that control. Tell Him that you have faith that He will bring something good out of this situation. Thank Him for already moving and working in your life.

This was going to take real concentration and effort on Jack's part, but it would eventually lead to an emotional independence that he had not experienced before.

All of us need to ask ourselves hard questions about the things we believe in and to think about the practical implications of those beliefs. For example, we were taught as children to live correctly. Now we need to take a good long look at old rules and regulations and challenge them. It helps to fill in the blanks in a statement such as "In my childhood home I was taught never to _____(argue)_____." Then challenge that statement by saying, "As I examine this rule for my own life, I _____(accept, reject)_____it. Instead I will learn to _____(speak up)_____."

It is important to shift that mindset of reaction to a mindset of initiative. That way, we can allow our behaviors to be inwardly guided rather than outwardly driven.

3. *Love Exchanges: Too Much or Too Little*

People do not naturally have the capacity to develop true independence unless they have had a foundation of balanced expressions of love throughout their developmental years. When we feel properly loved, our "batteries" are well charged, and we have a strong capacity to meet the trials of living without resorting to control tactics. Most imperative people feel insecure because they did not receive unconditional love from their parents.

On one extreme, I have counseled many imperative adults who are thoroughly frustrated because their current relationships do not meet the standards of an idealized past. These people report seemingly wonderful childhood experiences and relationships. I often find that they have such a high level of expectation that they are actually setting themselves up for disappointment. They entered adulthood so sure that there would be a continuation of ideal love that they could hardly handle anything short of perfection.

One woman told me, "My daddy would never have invalidated me the way my husband does. He was so wonderful! He was the perfect gentleman. I never heard a cross word from him in all my years at home."

A lack of love in childhood, the other extreme, is even more prevalent. Sharing love takes time, and many families simply have not committed themselves to the effort required. For example, a blank expression came over Jack's face when I asked him to describe the love in his early home. He told me, "I'm not saying my parents were unloving, but they didn't show their love by hugging me. They felt that was overdoing it, I think."

"Can you see the connection between the lack of

open expressions of love and your current demands for control in your own home?"

"I've never even thought about it," he replied.

"Think of it this way," I suggested. "Your irritabilities with your wife and children arise when you feel a lack of respect. Whether it is conscious or subconscious, I'm sure you think, 'I'm *not* going through my entire life without some respect from my family. I want people to show that they love me.' At that point you start telling them how to make your life easier.

"We all have a natural desire to be loved," I continued. "And when we don't receive that love, we become all the more intent on getting it."

Jack eventually realized that his critical nature was the result of his internal hunger for affirmation. During his younger years he had grown so impatient with the lack of love in his home, he had begun looking to outside sources to meet that need—the approval of his teachers and coaches, affection from a girlfriend. Then, still dissatisfied with the amount of love offered, he felt justified in demanding the affirmation he felt was rightfully his.

Whether their pasts gave them large doses of affirmation or minimal doses, it is unfair for imperative persons to place expectations on others because of those historical experiences. Instead, they can learn to acknowledge the fact that their current relationships are separate and distinct. For example, I encouraged Jack to learn to think of each member of his family as unique. He practiced making mental lists of the *ways* they were unique, and he thought about each person's positive traits. This led to a better understanding—and appreciation—of each person. With practice, he would be able to accept them the way they were, rather than expecting them to conform to his prototype.

4. *I Try Too Hard to Get My Way*

A consistent characteristic of imperative people is the desire to persuade others to be just like them. When encouraged to look back to their childhoods, most imperative people can recall a history of strong persuasion. Their parents may have been so intent on keeping order that their behavior said: "If I can get you to behave, then my world will be in order." The developmental years were full of relationships that featured arm-twisting, intimidation, or threats. Thus a model of dependent behavior was established and later integrated into the imperative person's lifestyle.

Jack told me that he had learned early on that it was not safe to be vulnerable. He told me, "I remember a scene when I was only five or six years old. I had just stepped onto the back porch of our home to set something outside when a very loud clap of thunder sounded. Scared to death, I ran indoors, where my father grabbed me and told me to quit acting so ridiculous. Then my mother scolded me for upsetting my father. I was immediately defensive and told them they were both mean. The next thing I knew, I was smarting from a spanking. They could be very forceful in communicating how I was supposed to act."

"In a sense, you were in school at times like that," I said. "You witnessed how effectively they persuaded you to be what they wanted, so you eventually learned to do likewise with your own family."

"I can see that you're right," he responded, "I do act that way with my wife and kids. I never thought about it much, but I can see where this is an unhealthy way to try to get along with other people."

While it is a good thing to express opinions (as opposed to repressing them), it is not healthy for us to become bossy or condescending or explosive in order to get our way.

For example, I told Jack, "When telling your wife that you'd like a few moments of relaxation, don't go on and on about how tired you are. This only creates antagonism, and it causes both of you to feed each other's bad moods. Simply state your need straightforwardly. Don't try to persuade or cajole. Keep an even tone of voice. This will show that your mood is not necessarily tied to her response."

5. *Mistakes Are Handled Heavy-handedly*

A woman once described to me a rotten day at work. A coworker had been pestering her all morning about minor problems that he could have resolved without her help. She was becoming more and more annoyed, so when she heard her office door opening one more time, without looking up she snapped, "Look, I just don't have time right now. You're going to have to . . ."

Just then her eyes met those of the senior vice president. Her first reaction was amusement, but it was immediately clear that he saw no humor in her error. He made a brief remark about her poor work ethic, then briskly left. Later that day she learned that he had filed a report, criticizing her insubordinate attitude. To make matters worse, he refused to tell her why he had come to her office in the first place.

Many of us can recall scenes, either in adulthood or childhood, when mistakes were blown out of proportion and handled in an ugly manner. While mistakes can actually be a prime opportunity for learning and introspection, they are often magnified to the extent that they create a chronically defensive mindset. When this is habitual, two things occur: (1) We become too fearful about the possibility of further episodes, and (2) we try harder than ever to be perfect.

Jack spoke with me once after he'd had a particularly stressful day. Like many people in the sales profession he complained, "I have to be so careful with my customers. Some people call in with the most unusual insurance claims. But if I'm not courteous, they either look for a new agent or they call my regional manager. I've been chewed out too many times, so I've learned to work extra hard to appease everyone. It drives me nuts!"

"I can appreciate that," I responded. "Certainly it adds to your stress level when part of your job is to please people." Suspecting that work was not his only immediate stressor, I then asked, "I wonder if you feel you have to be guarded in places other than work?"

"Oh, yeah. Lots of times I've felt like I couldn't share things at home with Claire. If she somehow gets a wrong impression, she might go hours without talking to me. She's not the yelling type, but that doesn't mean she's not unreasonable. Many times I've backed away from telling her about my personal struggles because I wanted to avoid a scene."

"And do you think this habit of defensiveness has any historical roots?"

"I'm sure it does. When I played football, I was specifically told, 'Don't do anything other than what we tell you.' If any of us guys made mistakes, we'd have to run extra laps or stay late for more practice.

"And I guess that was all very consistent with the way things were at home too," he continued. "I remember thinking my parents were experts at making mountains out of molehills!"

I mentioned to Jack that each of these situations was

accompanied with a lesson. "After you have experienced enough episodes where your mistakes involved greater consequences than necessary, you get edgy. The tendency to overreact is heightened. And the wish to make people stay within their prescribed limits also increases."

A healthier way to respond to bona fide errors is to discuss them calmly and openly. This kind of atmosphere is likely to heighten true understanding and influence. It is a slower process than the quick-fix, heavy-handed approach, yet in the long run it prevents wasted time due to repetitive tensions.

A major part of Jack's adjustment was in learning to exchange his imperative attitudes for healthier thoughts such as:

- "I can't afford to let other people dictate my moods. The way I respond is up to me."
- "I'm going to think about *why* I choose to behave calmly and fairly instead of in an overbearing manner."
- "Though I want and need love, I won't demand it."
- "I'll state my convictions clearly, then allow others the freedom to respond as they see fit."
- "We all make mistakes; nobody is perfect."

Jack learned that while it is normal for *some* moods to be influenced by circumstances, they certainly did not have to be controlled by circumstances. By depending less on the behavior of the people around him, he, in turn, was able to stop feeling the need to control that behavior. He began to appreciate how the allowance for separateness can increase the possibility for harmony.

CHAPTER 6

Do You Act Superior, Yet Feel Inferior?

In her mid-forties, Susan sought counseling because of long-standing anxiety problems. She was the mother of two teenagers, an eighteen-year-old son and a fifteen-year-old daughter. She and their father had divorced about nine years before, and she was currently married to a man several years older, who had two grown children and a grandchild. With two families demanding her attention, she was rarely at a loss for something to worry about. She told me she lived with a "be perfect" script, so she repeatedly bit off more activity than she could handle. Susan did not work outside the home, but she was very involved in several civic and church organizations.

Right away, in our first session, she spoke very openly about her reason for being in my office. "In the last couple of days I wrote down several things I wanted you to know," she told me. "I'd hate to think I'm sitting here wasting your time and mine by speaking in generalities." Before I had a chance to respond, she produced several sheets of paper and began reciting a detailed history of family tension.

Although her early home life had been free from excessive arguing, she had never felt very secure. Grades and proper etiquette had been her parents' priorities, particularly her mother's. And though Susan did fairly well in school, she always had the feeling that someone was looking over her shoulder to see if she was doing well enough! She had married a year out of college, but she and her first husband rarely got along.

"I wouldn't say he was an alcoholic," she told me, "but I grew up in a strict home with no liquor allowed and I found his drinking offensive. Plus, we fought about all sorts of things, from parenting to money to personal habits. I was a bundle of nerves. We should never have married in the first place. We were too different." They divorced after twelve years.

Four years went by before she married her current husband, Raymond. "He's a lot more mature and more sensitive than my first husband ever was. But I worry a lot about whether or not I can keep him happy. He's divorced too, but he has tried to keep very close ties with his kids, who are both married and live nearby. Sometimes I think he wants to cram too many things into his schedule, but I always go along with whatever he wants. I can tell you right now, it's not easy keeping up with him because I still have two teenagers who demand a lot of attention."

Wanting to know the specifics about her anxiety, I asked, "What things cause you the most tension?"

She told me that she worried a lot about what other people thought of her. When she made mistakes and other people found out about them, she was easily embarrassed. And she often brooded for days at a time over minor mishaps with friends. She confessed also that she was too critical with her children, but she quickly added that she loved them so much she just wanted the best for them. She reported having several bouts with headaches and intestinal disorders. And she complained that in spite of his normally pleasant disposition, Raymond seemed to tune her out whenever she talked about her various travails. This only made her feel worse, but she was reluctant to confront Raymond and tell him how she felt.

Early in our counseling sessions we focused on Susan's imperative thought patterns. Susan had a quick mind, so she was able to grasp how these things related to her anxiety feelings. Yet the anxiety did not go away quickly enough to please her. During one session she was telling me about an argument with her son, one of many stories that followed the same pattern.

"Susan," I told her, "a major reason you stay burdened by your personal problems is that you seem to be struggling with a real sense of inferiority. Your constant worry is a signal that you want to control your world in a way that will make you feel more adequate. But your efforts aren't succeeding. Every time you think you have failed, your negative emotions get stronger."

She raised an eyebrow in surprise and sounded a little indignant when she answered, "Well, I've always known that I have some insecurities, but I've never thought I had an inferiority complex!"

"Don't be too threatened by that word," I assured her. "When I talk about inferiority feelings, I'm referring to your constant need to measure up to what you think others expect of you. This feeling leaves you wondering if anyone approves of you. It can cause a lot of anxiety."

"I see what you mean," she said, "I guess my inferiority struggles—if we have to call them that—began when I was a girl. If my parents hadn't been so hard on me to perform well, I might not be in the shape I'm in now."

"Well, yes and no," I replied. "Surely your current feeling of inferiority has something to do with your parents' expectations, but we can't give all the credit to someone else. Actually, all people struggle with inferiority, no matter how good or bad their circumstances might have been. Much of our sense of inferiority is linked to our flawed human nature."

Identifying Your Inferiority Struggles

Imperative people often try to escape their inferiority feelings by trying to establish superiority over others. Most are not honest enough—or aware enough—to admit this openly. Yet their efforts at "one-upmanship" are so persistent that it is obvious they are trying to cover up any hint of their own personal inadequacies. Their inner tensions wouldn't exist if they enjoyed a sense of real personal security.

Sometimes the efforts to be superior are unmistakably clear, as in "You're never going to get my respect until you measure up to my standards." Clearly recognized "superior" traits like bossiness, intimidation, arrogance, or a "know-it-all" attitude accompany these obvious efforts. Imperative people often seem to be thinking, *I don't know why people are so dumb,* or *You just can't depend on anyone these days.*

Other times, imperative people are not quite so abrasive in declaring their superiority, but they send subtle messages just the same. They are baffled by the apparent nonsense in other people's decisions or behaviors, yet they may disguise their disdain, thereby hiding their inner conflicts. Some of the disguised efforts to be superior include defensiveness, passive noncompliance, perfectionism, and moral martyrdom.

Whatever form the superiority takes, imperative people ensure perpetual tension by behaving this way. There is no possible way to establish moral superiority over another person because at the core of our being, all of us are equally guilty of sin and equally valued by God. When imperative people don't understand this, they become entangled in all sorts of emotional snares.

To determine the extent to which you might be ensnared by this problem, respond to the following statements that describe you:

_____ **"My emotions are easily aroused when someone tries to make me look foolish."**

_____ **"When talking about myself, I only reveal what is positive, not what is negative."**

_____ **"When my flaws are discussed by others, I respond by pointing out their flaws."**

_____ **"I am comfortable in my environment only after I put everything in its proper place."**

_____ **"I deliberately avoid talking to people who do not fit my social status."**

_____ **"When expressing limits to children or subordinates, I have been known to speak sharply."**

If you checked three or more of the above statements, your imperative thoughts are unnecessarily pushing you to deny your humanness and feign superiority.

The Root of Inferiority Feelings

It would be inaccurate to say that environmental strains are the sole cause of inferiority. Although many of us (Susan included) can recall unpleasant past experiences that undercut our feelings of personal adequacy, *our inferiority would exist even if we only had delightful experiences*. When we say, "Nobody's perfect," we're telling the truth.

Inside each one of us is a God-given awareness of basic right and wrong. This is accompanied by the uneasy knowledge that we do not possess the capacity to live perfect lives. Some people find this idea so foreign they do not consciously grapple with it. Their struggle remains on the unconscious level. Other individuals, who are more psychologically or spiritually inclined, are willing to admit their personal inadequacies, yet they don't really understand that feelings of inferiority can cause us to project an image of ourselves that we can't live up to.

Evidences of our inborn inclination toward inferiority begin in childhood. Most children are shy with new people. They tend to hide their mistakes. Children think, *People might not accept me if they knew the truth about me.*

Adults also show evidences of inferiority struggles. We defensively keep from exposing our secret sins. We become envious when peers achieve success. Even when our mistakes are glaringly obvious, we have a hard time admitting we are wrong. When someone tells a personal success story, we immediately try to match it with one of our own. Hardly a day goes by that we don't compare ourselves with others.

Accepting Inferiority While Feigning Superiority

In general, there are two ways people tend to respond to feelings of inferiority.

1. *Accepting Inferiority*

The first response is to give up and accept our unworthiness as a given. This leads us to let the reminders of our past failures and unmet aspirations hold us down. Susan and I discussed how she often became her own worst enemy. "You really fret unnecessarily about your okay-ness," I told her.

"I'm afraid you're right," Susan replied. "I can't stand to make mistakes. I know I have capabilities, but for some reason my life keeps getting sidetracked by one annoyance after another. I never seem to feel as if I'm reaching my full potential."

"Can you give me an example of what you're talking about?"

"I sure can. There is one part of my past that seems to be a millstone around my neck," she confessed. "From the time I was a little girl, I wanted to be a teacher. So you can imagine how thrilled I was when I got a teaching job right out of college. I was determined to be the best teacher in my school, but after I had been on the job for just three years, I had some major problems with a hardheaded principal. He was totally unreasonable in his expectations, and I was constantly missing his mandated deadlines. Finally, he told me my contract wouldn't be renewed. Les, I was *fired* from the job I wanted to do more than anything in the world!"

"I'm sure someone must have told you this wasn't the end of the world."

"Oh, lots of people told me it wasn't my fault. He was an impossible man to work for. But *still*. It's a blot on my record that can't ever be erased!"

Taking an educated guess, I asked, "Susan, can I assume that you respond to most failures with some pretty harsh self-talk?"

"Oh, I suppose so. I know I'm my own toughest critic, but I can't seem to help it. When I don't succeed, I feel like the worst kind of failure. And I can't seem to stop thinking about the mess I've made."

Individuals like Susan assume very early in life that they can conquer their feelings of inadequacy only if they perform well enough. So when a stain spoils their performance record, they feel they have no choice but to put a demerit mark on their value rating.

Susan and I talked about ways we can counteract this habit. Instead of grading ourselves down for each mistake, we can learn to say things like:

- The sun came up this morning even though I ___
        (put a dent in the car yesterday)   .
- Our dinner guests had a good time even though I
        (spilled coffee on the tablecloth)
- My husband still loves me even though I _____
        (forgot to get his cleaning)
- I feel good about myself even though _____
        (the house is a mess)

2. *Feigning Superiority*

The second response to the natural struggle with inferiority is to attempt to become falsely superior. Imperative people are convinced that if they can make other people seem less adequate, they will somehow enhance their own worth. Therefore they elevate themselves at someone else's expense.

I told Susan that if she was like most people, she probably didn't allow herself to remain on the bottom of the heap very long. Whether premeditated or not, it was likely that she used many different techniques to gain the upper hand.

Intrigued by this idea, Susan asked, "What are the clues? How do I know if I'm trying to act superior?"

"Well, Susan, you mentioned earlier that you don't have any patience with other people's quirks. Being critical is one way to stroke your own ego. When you focus on someone else's flaws, you don't have time to think about your own."

"You sure are touching a sore spot," she admitted. "I've known since childhood that I needed to ease up on my critical thoughts. But I've never really considered how they were tied to a false attempt to overcome inferiority."

"Take perfectionism, for example. Even though a perfectionist knows that life can't be flawless, he has a compelling drive to be perfect.

Susan nodded. "Let me ask you something. Is the silent treatment an attempt to be superior? My husband tells me I try to gain unfair advantage by refusing to speak to him."

"He's right. The person using the silent treatment is usually thinking, *I may not be able to argue as well as you, but I can win this round if I refuse to talk.*"

By nature, humans are competitive. And even if we accept the proposition that inferiority is intrinsic to each of us, most of us will not want to stay on the lowest rung of the ladder without first trying to be "one-up." Since imperative people are driven by inner performance requirements, they are especially hungry to maintain a competitive edge.

How About You?

Take a moment to see if you are using any of these false superiority tactics:

_____ **"I use sarcasm to undercut an opposing point of view."**

_____ **"I find myself stubbornly clinging to old behaviors rather than trying changes someone else has suggested."**

_____ "I hate to admit it's my fault when misunder-
standings occur."

_____ "I've been known to downgrade someone behind
his back."

_____ "I often give unsolicited advice."

_____ "Sometimes I ask questions that I know will make
the other person look foolish."

If you checked two of the above statements, you are
engaged in a race to beat the next guy. These tactics,
however, only create an illusion of superiority.

Myths That Perpetuate the Struggle

When I counsel imperative people like Susan, I explain that they don't need to play this inferior-superior
game. Though each of us possesses different skills and
weaknesses, our intrinsic value is the same. When we
can accept this idea, we lose the need for controlling
and "one-upping" each other. But to live with equality, it
is necessary to eliminate some common myths.

Myth #1: Weaknesses Have to Be Secrets

I instructed Susan to maintain a simple belief: those
who can show weakness reveal their strength. There is
nothing heroic about maintaining an image of being
above it all. Each one of us is a mixed bag of pluses and
minuses, and the person who cannot tolerate public
knowledge of both strengths and weaknesses is
weighted down by phoniness.

When I talked with Susan about her difficulty in re-
vealing personal weaknesses, it became plain that I had
touched a raw nerve. Not at all comfortable with the
idea of feeling exposed, she nervously said, "Surely you
can appreciate what would happen to my reputation if I

suddenly disclosed all of my hang-ups. I've worked hard to develop good friendships and a good reputation. I just can't tell people all about my fears and insecurities. Besides, why do they need to know?"

"Let me share with you one of my basic beliefs," I answered. "I believe all people have similar inner battles with emotions and attitudes. We all struggle with these tensions. This puts us on even ground with one another. If I refuse to admit my humanness, I'm being dishonest by portraying myself as something I am not."

"Well, I agree with you there, but I'd still feel funny telling my friends how hard I struggle with anxiety," Susan rebutted. "I don't think they'd understand."

"I don't mean going around town airing all your problems," I said. "There's a big difference, Susan, between confessing on a soap box and being willing to admit to certain weaknesses in a natural way. For example, next time you make a mistake, you don't have to try to cover it up. Instead, you can smile and say, 'Oh, look what I did!' Your friends might be relieved to find out that you're not as perfect as you were leading them to believe."

Myth #2: Perfection Is a Cure for Inferiority

Inferiority is an *internal* issue, so it requires internal solutions. When imperative people try to overcome inferiority by making themselves look good, the result is a window-dressing approach to problem solving.

Nobody said that internal changes are easy. They do not come quickly. They require contemplation and prayer. Our minds are not always willing to shift gears—even when the changes required are obvious. Therefore, many imperative people reject the idea of resolving internal problems with internal solutions. Instead they think, *If I can seem to be above it all, if I can fit my world into a tidy mold, if I can be in control—this will prove beyond all doubt that I'm superior!*

Susan's efforts at superiority were displayed in her attempts to control her own emotions and in attempts to control the emotions and feelings of family members. She once confessed, "I feel so abnormal when I have strong emotions I'm not supposed to have. Sometimes I feel anger, hate, resentment—and I absolutely cannot allow these." Later, it was no surprise to me when she also admitted that she continually tried to force her husband and children to refrain from expressing their unpleasant emotions.

"Susan, by trying to maintain perfection in your emotions and your family's, you are guaranteeing an increase in tension. I believe that no person this side of heaven will ever become perfect. By expecting so much of yourself, you're setting yourself up to feel more inferior than ever."

Perfectionism is not a solution to inferiority. It is a sure path to increased problems. Either it results in extra guilt and anger when a situation cannot be remedied, or it creates a false sense of arrogance when it appears that the standard has been successfully attained.

Instead of seeking perfection as a cure for inferiority, Susan—and those like her—learned to pay attention when her negative emotions appeared. She learned to say, "Stop!" to those emotions and immediately give priority to realistic thoughts.

Myth #3: Inferiority Is Relieved by Keeping Others Satisfied

I recall a recent conversation with a woman who had just sung a solo in her church. Before singing she felt insecure because she was performing an unfamiliar number. But she was a gifted performer, and after the song was completed, she was greeted with enthusiastic remarks. She overcame her insecurity by pleasing the crowd.

Imperative people can recall times when they were sure they could resolve their uneasy feelings if only they could make others happy. For example, Susan told me, "I'm so anxious when my fifteen-year-old daughter gets ready to go out with her friends. She gets annoyed at my hovering, but I can't help feeling the way I do. So I've fallen into a trap of trying to make sure everything goes just right for her. If she can have a good time, I feel an inner peace." Susan was saying that she felt good about herself only if her daughter thought she was a wonderful mother.

Two problems erupt when we try *too* hard to keep others appeased. First, we feel unstable because it's impossible to keep others continually happy. Second, we grow impatient with ourselves because we aren't successful in making others think and feel "correctly."

It is impossible to resolve inferiority feelings by satisfying others. Instead of pushing so hard to meet arbitrary standards, imperative people can find the stability they seek by learning to be content through spiritual growth. When this happens, inner desire rather than an outside "must" will motivate their behavior. Excellence can still be pursued—but not as a means to attain false superiority.

Although Susan's initial reason for counseling was her anxiety, she grew to understand that her inferiority-superiority struggle was at the root of her problems. Armed with this new insight, she was able to diminish her imperative tendencies with a new set of guiding thoughts:

- "It's normal to let others see who I really am."
- "People-pleasing behavior does not solve my problems."
- "If someone chooses to fault me for being human, I have no need to give undue attention to it."
- "When I make a mistake, I don't have to cover it up."
- "Trying to act as if I'm superior to other people does nothing to build my self-esteem."
- "My self-worth is a given; it does not have to be earned."

CHAPTER 7

Do You Have an Inborn Craving for Control?

Duty, dependency, inferiority—all are pieces of the puzzle that form the foundation of our imperative personalities. Often these are variables, which may or may not have affected a particular person. But another piece of the puzzle, though often overlooked, is *always* present in all of us: *our inborn craving for control.*

Even with the insights Bob Wright had developed as he attended counseling sessions, he still realized that he needed to understand something more about himself. Half-anguished, half-joking, he confided, "I can't seem to be rid of my imperative thoughts for any time at all. At work, at home, with my friends, I'm always aware of wanting to be in control. I think I'm doing a little better job at harnessing my tongue, but this control issue seems to permeate my whole personality. I'm beginning to think it always has."

"Do you mean that you can look back over all your forty-two years and see that you've had the same tendencies throughout your life?"

"Yeah, something like that. I remember as a boy I was often stubborn. When I disagreed with my parents, I would outwardly go along with them to keep out of trouble, but inwardly I kept on thinking just what I wanted to." His eyes twinkled as he added, "My ideas were invariably better than theirs.

"And do you know what?" he went on. "I see my two sons having the same tendencies today. They have their own opinions, and they don't like Mom or Dad horning in on their lifestyle. Maybe this is a family trait that we've been passing on from one generation to the next."

"Bob, I agree that there are undoubtedly some family tendencies at work here, and we can examine those later. But you're putting your finger on something that's much larger than a learned tendency. You're becoming aware of one of the universal flaws of human nature."

Heaving a mock sigh of relief, Bob declared, "Well, at least it's comforting to know that there are others out there like me. I'd hate to think I was one of the few who have to struggle with these urges to control."

"Let's take a close look at something," I said. "Try to imagine some of the most common problems in our daily lives. You know . . . things like impatience, insecurity, insensitivity, lack of communication. If you had to identify the single trait common to all of these issues, what would you choose?"

Bob reflected a moment, then said, "The only thing that comes to mind is that each of the problems you just mentioned indicates some amount of selfishness. Is it possible that when we get hooked into troublesome reactions, our *self* is our primary concern?"

"You've hit the nail on the head," I told him. "When you get right down to the essence of what causes us to get off track in unhealthy living, self-oriented thinking always seems to be at the root of it."

"Well, wait a minute. *Always* is a pretty strong word," Bob cautioned. "Are you willing to go that far out on the limb to say that self-oriented thoughts are involved in troubled behavior every single time?"

"I sure am. I believe it is impossible for a person to truly behave inappropriately unless he is pushed along by self-preoccupied thoughts. The desire to put self first is intrinsic to human nature. And this desire is manifested in a multitude of ways."

"Les, I've heard ministers speak about the troubles that come from putting yourself first, but I never thought much about it once church was over. If this belief of yours is true, I'm going to have to think about it a whole lot."

"Let's just pick a few common emotional and behavioral problems and I'll show you what I mean," I urged him. "For example, we all find it easy to be critical. What's at the base of that trait?"

"That's pretty easy," Bob replied. "When we're being critical, we seem to be focusing on the other person, but we're really zeroing in on *my* ideas, *my* preferences. I can't say I've ever really looked for "self" at the heart of criticism, but I'll bet it's always there."

"And you'd probably also agree that criticism then leads to such problems as impatience, bossiness, irritability, envy, anger. These emotions are all fed by self-oriented thinking."

Bob nodded.

"Now let's consider some more subtle traits. For example, you may get your feelings hurt too easily and sulk. Or you may disagree with someone's point of view and become judgmental. Or maybe you're so wrapped up in a work project that you forget to do a favor your wife requested. In each of these cases self-preoccupied thinking is at the core."

"I see what you mean."

"Actually, I could go on and on. Many other problems reflect this tendency. Infatuation, rebellion, procrastination, resentment, worry, social withdrawal, excessive talking. Each in its own way indicates that the mind is overloaded with considerations about *me*."

"Wow. This is no minor matter," Bob concluded. "You've helped me identify how easily I get caught up in imperative thinking. But I still don't understand why the craving for control should be a fact of human nature."

It was then that I began to discuss the Garden of Eden with Bob.

Understanding Human Nature

Individuals have been struggling with the desire for control since the Garden of Eden. Prior to the introduction of sin, Adam and Eve had no conflict. We can assume that their relationship was filled with many positive experiences—understanding, patience, encouragement, gentleness, love. Living fully within the image of God, they were not consumed with the desire for dominance over one another, but sought instead to find ways to serve, to stimulate, to reinforce each other.

God had been generous in His gifts to this couple. He gave them a home in Paradise, made sure their physical needs were taken care of, and gave them enjoyable work to do. His rules were simple and straightforward: "From any tree of the garden you may eat freely; but from the Tree of Knowledge of Good and Evil you shall not eat." In other words, they were gifted with freedom, and they had an abundance of choices. But they would use this freedom best when they balanced it with submission to God's declarations of right and wrong. God had given them an inner conscience to guide their free choices.

By the time Adam and Eve appeared on the scene, Satan and his cohorts had already rebelled against God. Having attempted to make himself "like the Most High," Satan and his army had been thrust out of heaven and were now wandering the earth. Certainly Satan viewed Adam as an adversary. After all, God had created a new being and clothed him with His own image. So Satan devised a scheme to turn Adam (and thereby the descendants he represented) away from God. Knowing of God's instruction to submit to His rules, Satan went right to work on Eve. He must have figured that if he could turn her away from God, Adam would surely follow suit.

Satan, the serpent, is described as being more crafty than any beast of the field. He knew he could not gain a foothold in Adam and Eve's minds by launching an all-out smear campaign against God. So he settled on a much more subtle, seductive strategy. He enticed them with the idea of *self*. Beginning with the question, "Has God said . . . ?" he put doubt in Eve's mind that God was as all-knowing as she had previously believed.

Eve's mind began to spin. "I've never thought to question God. But maybe I should. After all, I *do* know a few things."

Having put his foot in the door, Satan kept pushing. "You don't think God would actually punish you for living according to your own convictions, do you? Think about it, Eve. You're as smart as He is. You have good sense. If your notions are a little different from God's, so what? You have every right to follow your own ideas of right and wrong. Be your own god!"

By agreeing to eat of the Tree of Knowledge of Good and Evil, Eve symbolically endorsed the philosophy "Life is best lived when I am in control."

Once Eve succumbed, she immediately appealed to Adam, who readily joined her rebellion. And so imperative thinking was born. Self-knowledge and self-importance overcame humanity. Enamored as they were with the possibility of being as high as God, what mattered most to these two was being correct, being in charge, being as God.

As a result, the Lord set into motion a system of consequences communicating His displeasure. Adam and Eve were relegated to a lower, tension-filled way of life. They were allowed to cling to their self-preoccupation, which, in fact, became integral to their personalities. But they soon found this to be a matter of torment rather than delight. And since Adam and Eve represented all humanity, their descendants were doomed to be born with this inclination. The prophet Isaiah summarized the situation by stating, "Each of us has turned to his own way."[1]

Bob and I discussed at great length the implications of the human desire for self-importance. He told me, "I've known the Garden of Eden story since I was in grade school, but I've never really thought about its meaning. It sure never had much impact on my understanding of human nature. I just assumed they had eaten some bad apples!" Bob laughed at his own joke.

"What happened in that garden was far more than a decision to eat fruit," I commented. "The issue of control was at stake. Would control of the personality be surrendered to God or would self assume it? Unfortunately, the promise of self-control proved too alluring, and Adam and Eve made the wrong decision.

"The New Testament makes it clear that we are each *in Adam*," I continued. "That means we're all born with the same cravings that he possessed. No one has to teach us to be selfish."

Bob reflected, "I see what you mean. By *selfish* you imply that each person naturally wants to be in control of his own life. I can sure identify with that." He thought about it a minute, then went on. "Les, I must say that your perspective is far different from secular psychologists'. Most of them would lead people to believe that personality problems are caused by bad parenting or unfortunate circumstances. You are making psychology a matter of spirituality."

"That's exactly what it is, Bob. Primarily we have emotional and behavioral problems *not* because of our upbringing but because of indwelling sin. Certainly we can each recall unwelcome experiences that increased our personal tensions. But our ultimate problem is our spiritual disease."

The Need for Control Is a Spiritual Issue

I asked Bob about the atmosphere in his childhood home. "I'm not going to kid you by saying my home was perfect, but it wasn't bad either," he replied. "I had a pretty normal childhood. I've got to give my parents credit because, in spite of some mistakes, they did all they could to teach me good values."

My curiosity was aroused, and I asked, "How would you describe each of your parents?"

Bob smiled as he began. "Oh, I guess you could say that my dad had some Archie Bunker in him. He could be a bit opinionated, and sometimes I thought his ideas, especially about the way he thought I ought to act, were too old-fashioned. But deep down he was a teddy bear. I remember how he'd like to sit with me and my brother and laugh about some of the tomfoolery that guys like to talk about. He was sometimes strict, but all-in-all we had a good relationship.

"Mom and I weren't extremely close. We weren't distant or unfriendly; it's just that she never had any brothers and wasn't interested in sports. She was always around the house when I came in from school or from playing ball. We didn't talk much except about household chores and that sort of thing. I guess you could say I took her pretty much for granted."

Bob and I then spoke for several more minutes about how his parents made sure he was in church, insisted on good grades, taught him right from wrong. Bob concluded, "It seems to me my childhood was a lot better than most."

Wanting to remind Bob that his character was more than the sum of his childhood experiences, I responded, "Bob, I didn't know you when you were two years old, but I can take a guess at some of the ways you acted. I suspect you were known to cry when you were told it was time to stop playing. And you probably clung to your toys if a friend wanted to play with them. You may have even thrown a temper tantrum when your mother said you had to eat your vegetables before you could have dessert."

A grin flashed across his face. "I guess I'll have to plead guilty to your charges. In fact, I'm sure I did a lot more than those few things."

I grinned with him, then went on. "You were fortunate to have parents who gave you a good foundation. Yet something deeper than just trained tendencies was at work in you as a child. Your inborn spirit was, and is, inclined to go your own way in spite of the good values given you."

Whether our environment is pleasant or distasteful, the craving to be in control still looms within us. Ultimately, imperative tendencies cannot be altered until the individual accepts responsibility for his actions and decides to change. Interestingly, when biblical passages instruct us to set aside controlling behavior in favor of kindness or humility, they are never followed by the phrase "... that is, if you had a good childhood." Biblical writers were not insensitive to environmental problems. Rather, they were aware that problematic behaviors and attitudes exist regardless of background. Therefore, all wrongful living and all attempts to make healthy corrections are ultimately matters to be settled between God and ourselves.

The Implications of Being Naturally Sinful

By tracing the origins of controlling behavior to the decision to "be as God," imperative people can develop a better understanding of their own daily actions and emotions. An important step in overcoming imperative tendencies is to be keenly aware of who we are.

Each Person Has Some Insensitivities

We generally think of an insensitive person as being very abrasive, aloof, inattentive, and aggressive, but insensitivity is often conveyed in less obvious ways: tardiness, evasiveness, laziness, or tuning out, for instance.

Sometimes insensitivity is clearly deliberate, but imperative people are often insensitive without realizing it.

Bob once told me, "I'm sure I can minimize my obviously abrasive habits, but my hardest job will be to keep an eye on my more subtle attempts at control. Sometimes Elaine gets annoyed with me, and I can't see why. I'm not even aware that I've done something aggravating. When she points it out, I'll usually realize I was wrong, but I often don't catch myself until it's too late."

"Can you think of an example?"

"Sure. Just last night she asked me to check on Chad to see if he was getting his homework done. I said I would, but I got sidetracked on a project in the garage and completely forgot about it. An hour later she bawled me out for neglecting the kids and complained that I left too much of the parenting to her."

"So she felt controlled by your neglect, even though you hadn't consciously tried to control her."

"That's right. And unfortunately those kinds of incidents aren't rare. Sometimes I get so absorbed in what I'm doing, I forget the way I might be affecting other people."

Bob took a giant step forward when he realized it is human nature to think of oneself and neglect other people's needs. He knew it was possible to change, but it was going to require real concentration since he had hardly ever been challenged to analyze this side of himself.

Letting Go of Control Is Not Natural

I have been an achiever my entire life. In my early years I was immersed in this philosophy: "Learn what your responsibilities are and do them well." It meant if I had a school assignment or a chore at home, I had to figure the best and most efficient way to get it done so I would have time to play ball or visit a friend. I wanted all the loose ends of my life to be tied down. To this day I'm not comfortable when I have more activities to do than time will allow. I like being in control of my world. At its best, this mindset gives me organizational skills. At its worst, it creates stress since my world does not always cooperate with my wishes.

Certainly it is good to be responsible for the obligations of living. Yet virtually every person has to struggle to discover the delicate balance between healthy achievement and self-preoccupied performance. The inborn desire to be in charge keeps popping out. Some people try to control time commitments. Others control their surroundings by constantly making things neat and clean around them. Still others try to control public opinion by manipulating and slanting the facts. Intellectually, we may know very well that we cannot satisfy all our cravings, yet we proceed as if we can create precisely the order we require.

Bob was becoming painfully aware of the impossibility of casually putting this mindset aside. He told me, "I've been trying to ease up on criticism and impatience in my dealings with other people, but it sure hasn't been easy! Even when I *am* able to put the brakes on, I still find my thoughts leaning toward that old controlling behavior. I wonder if I'll ever be able to break this habit completely."

Knowing from personal experience what he was feeling, I assured him, "Your admission that you still have thoughts of control is a good first step toward improvement. The more you're aware of how powerful the control trait is in your personality, the better your ability to let it go."

"I'm encouraged to hear you say that," Bob replied. "I've wondered if I could ever get a grip on the problem."

"Let me confess something to you, Bob. I've put a lot of effort into gaining insight into my own flawed character. And I've often thought that I would have fewer problems if the people in my world would arrive at the same insights that I have. But therein lies a snag. All other people possess a human nature that craves control, but not everyone cares to remedy the problem. So it's easy for me to revert to the idea that if they don't change, I won't try to change either!"

Very few things in life come with a guarantee. But one thing is for sure. Until the day we enter heaven, each person will in some way contend with self-preoccupation to some extent. We can try to improve, but if we are honest, we will admit that we have a weak spot that tempts us to revert to imperative ways. Just as a person may be able to move from one culture to another and learn a new language and live a different style of life, but never forget the old ways, so imperative people can learn a way of life that is more relaxed and accepting, but there will always be a remnant of the old intrinsic traits.

We Are Each Responsible for Internal Changes

By tying imperative living to human nature, I mean to emphasize the fact that personal growth can only originate from within. Imperative people will change only as they realize that (1) externals will not fit into a tidy package, and (2) even if they did, inner peace would not be a natural result.

Bob shared a moment of real insight with me. "Actually, Les, when I compare my life with that of most other men, I have to admit that I've got it pretty good. In spite of my problems at home, I know Elaine loves me. And I have to give her credit for trying to be cooperative most of the time. And my sons are way above average. They've provided plenty of annoyances, but they're really good kids. They don't drink alcohol or use drugs. They have good morals, and so do the kids they go around with. My job is steady. I have all my real needs met. When I think it through, I realize I'm spoiled. Maybe one of the definitions of a spoiled person is not knowing when to be satisfied."

"Bob, I'm sure that we could make a list of changes in your home that would make you feel more at ease, but I'm hearing you admit that that's not the point. You're saying that you can only find emotional balance as you learn to more carefully monitor your inner thoughts and reactions." (This process is discussed fully in Three Steps toward Changed Thinking in chapter 9.)

"Yeah. But as simple as that is to say, it's still hard for me to do. All my life I've been trying to make others fit my standards. But my focus is shifting. I know that even if everyone in the world kowtows to my demands, I'll still have to confront my inner self before I'm at peace."

Persons fully given to imperative living are like the proverbial horse chasing the dangling carrot. They are trying to find a life that will never be. They are refusing to acknowledge the inevitability of their world's imperfections.

But by identifying and understanding the innate struggle with prideful self-preoccupation, people like Bob can begin embracing healthier, less imperative thoughts like:

- "I want to be more aware of other people's feelings and needs."
- "I realize I can't expect everything to turn out just the way I want it."
- "I am responsible for my decisions; I choose not to blame others."
- "I am committed to the struggle to relinquish control."

By identifying his inclination toward prideful thinking, Bob was learning a major fact about personal transformation. It comes not by adjusting the externals, but by realigning deepest beliefs. Bob's breakthrough began as he learned to recognize the link between his imperative lifestyle and his thought world.

When imperative thinking burdens us with an overwhelming sense of duty, makes us unnecessarily dependent on other people's responses, exhausts us with attempts to appear superior, and frustrates us with the constant need to be in control, we embark on a never-ending cycle of negative emotions and experiences. Can you free yourself from this destructive pattern? The answer is *yes!* The elements that contribute to your imperative personality can be conquered. Part Three will show you how you can be free to be who you are and at the same time walk humbly with your Lord.

PART THREE

Yielding and Being Liberated

CHAPTER 8

Being Free to Be Who You Are

Jack, the former football player with the bad temper, knew something needed to change if he was to gain emotional control. Although he was a successful insurance salesman, he was under a great deal of stress trying to keep both his clients and management happy. His wife had told me he was impossible to live with, and she was threatening divorce. Jack was eager to keep his family intact, and though he hadn't really wanted to get counseling, now he was feeling encouraged by it. My previous discussions with him about his dependencies had caught him off guard since he had always prided himself on being so independent. Yet, when he really took a good, honest look at himself, he had to admit that he was often angry when people didn't live up to his expectations. He could only feel that his world was in order when others acted the way he wanted them to.

"Les, I know I shouldn't let my feelings be controlled by circumstances," he told me, "but I guess I'm overly concerned about my family. I'm really having a hard time feeling relaxed when they do things that aren't good."

"Can you give me an example?" I asked.

"Well, my teenage daughter is too argumentative with my wife, Claire. Whenever Claire asks her to do a simple thing like cleaning up the kitchen, it turns into a big fight. In my mind I can hear you telling me not to let the circumstances dictate my mood, but at the same time I can't let my daughter talk this way to her mother."

I pointed out the irony of the situation. "You get hooked into being angry because you want the best for your daughter. You and she both might be less agitated if you didn't know what was right."

"Yeah, I know." He shook his head. "But I can't just let her do whatever she wants to do. We'd have nothing but chaos around our house."

"Let's stop and consider something," I said. "You don't want chaos in your home. I can appreciate that. . . . But I wonder what might happen if you eased up on your harsh requirements. Do you suppose the family would come apart at the seams?"

Jack hesitated. "Well, I'm sure not going to adopt an 'anything goes' philosophy, if that's what you mean. In my house we *will* have order."

"I don't have any problem with that," I told him. "But how about establishing order without excessive tension?"

Jack looked relieved. "That sounds okay to me. How do we do that?"

"Let's consider a new thinking pattern—one that's the opposite of imperative thinking. In this new pattern we'll throw away dogmatism and rigidity and become anchored in something very different . . . thoughts of *freedom* instead of thoughts of control."

Jack sat up straight in his chair. "*Free*dom! You expect

me to let my wife and kids roam free, doing whatever in this world they want? Do you realize what that might lead to?"

"Jack, I realize this much . . . so far your control tactics have brought a great strain on you and your family. A couple of weeks ago your wife threatened to leave you. You have to admit that you've been pretty unhappy. It's time for a change. If you can get a good handle on what freedom is all about, I'm sure you can move your family in a more positive direction."

"Okay, okay. You've made your point." He settled back in his chair. "But you've got some explaining to do."

"Let me begin by giving an analogy. Have you ever kept a dog around the house?"

A curious look crossed his face, and his head leaned to one side. "Well, yeah. I had a dog when I was a kid."

"Good, then you'll be able to relate to this. Let's say your dog lives his entire life fenced in the backyard. You're a good owner. You feed him well, you play ball with him, you occasionally let him indoors. But each day this dog realizes he's stuck behind that fence. What thought is predominant in the dog's mind?"

Jack grinned as he answered. "No dog has ever talked to me. At least I wouldn't admit it for fear you'd put me away. But I'd say that dog is thinking about getting out."

"Let's put it this way," I said. "When that gate swings open, you won't see that dog *walk* out. He's gone!" We both chuckled as we pictured the scene in our minds.

"People can be very much like that," I continued. "When they live day in, day out behind someone else's fence of regulations, they eventually look for the escape hatch. Those who get out are often rebellious. Those who remain trapped can become bitter or depressed."

"So you're telling me that if I continue to be too demanding, I'll lose my family."

"That's exactly what I'm saying. No one likes to be fenced in. Sooner or later, they'll begin looking for the gate to freedom."

Jack nodded. He thought for a moment about how he was slowly but surely losing his three children and Claire. "Okay, I'm hearing you so far."

"Now picture in your mind an old country dog," I continued. "He has no fence around him, just wide open spaces. He enjoys the freedom a city dog can never know."

Jack smiled and said, "My uncle used to have a lot of land, and he had a dog like that. I loved going to his place because it was so peaceful."

"Now let me ask you, Jack, have you ever known a tense, uptight country dog?"

"Of course not! Ol' Buster, my uncle's dog, was the most friendly dog you ever saw. I don't guess he ever got flustered about anything."

"And when you went to look for him, I'll bet he was right up on the porch, wasn't he?"

"He sure was. Are you suggesting that the way to cause others to come close to me is to let them have some space?"

"That's what I'm suggesting. When you give freedom to others, it doesn't mean you are lowering your standards or that you don't care about them. It means you are providing an atmosphere to let others think and feel and act without excessive pressure to fit your mold. The paradox is that when others sense the freedom you offer, they are *more* attracted to you. The key is to learn how to use this freedom."

I Like Freedom, But . . .

In the recent past, world news has been full of stories about people who are courageously claiming the right to free rule. We Americans have applauded these heroic citizens. We have boldly asserted that no dictator, no system has the right to refuse individuals their God-given liberty. Our own country's history is anchored in the right to be free from any despot's rule. We have established a national holiday to celebrate the inauguration of freedom in our land, and on that day we brim with national pride as we commemorate the bedrock principle that has made America great. We love freedom! Or do we?

In my years of counseling I have discovered that many people embrace the concept of freedom as long as it remains abstract or as long as it does not require personal adjustments. But when I challenge them to give freedom to their own family members or to be freer in admitting their real emotions, many flinch.

How about you? Are you afraid to give freedom to those around you? Check the statements that apply to you.

_____ "I know I should give my husband the freedom to be who he is, *but* I'm not sure he's trustworthy."

_____ "It would be good to let my wife have more free reign in household decisions, *but* she has no common sense."

_____ "I want to feel free to let others see the real me, *but* I'm not sure I'll be accepted."

_____ "My kids should feel free to be themselves, *but* they'd better do as I say."

These contradictions—and many similar ones—
indicate that you are hedging on freedom. Why is this?

Let's get a perspective by returning to our spiritual
roots. In chapter 7 we learned that an understanding of
imperative tendencies can be found by analyzing the
Garden of Eden. Prior to Adam's fall, God had offered
the simple instruction: "From any tree of the garden you
may eat *freely,* but from the Tree of Knowledge of Good
and Evil you shall not eat." Mankind was intended by
God to be free, and this freedom would be best balanced
by submission to God's ways.

It was the decision to "be as God" that threw Adam's
life out of balance. He liked the idea of freedom, but
he wanted it without any strings attached. Even after
Adam's rebellion, God chose not to rescind freedom.
Rather than coercing mankind to return to Him, He still
gave us the gift of choice. As a result, freedom became
somewhat risky. For there is no guarantee that any person can be fully trusted to do what is right. This sets up
the conflict: we want to be free, but we are afraid to
allow others that same freedom—someone might abuse
it.

This fear is very evident in issues that are close to our
personal needs. The more meaningful a thing is to us,
the more we are tempted to try to control it. For example, most of us marry with the idea that this union will
be the core of our present and future happiness. Sometimes we so strongly want the relationship to be a
good one that we try to force our partners into a pattern of our own choosing. We don't permit different
ideas or feelings since these might threaten our own
happiness.

In much the same way we have high expectations for
our children. We so strongly want to feel successful as
parents that we demand very specific behaviors and at-

titudes from our young. The idea of letting children have choices is unsettling. It might disrupt our own plans for them.

Likewise, in the world of work, at church, in civic organizations, we can have such a powerful drive to succeed that we hesitate to allow others to be who they are. We are afraid they might make a poor decision or create a bad impression for the group. To prevent problems, we take control.

Indeed, our fears can be legitimate. What person has not been disappointed at the decisions or actions of another? It would be foolhardy to think that all people will always use freedom responsibly. Yet as risky as freedom is, the imperative, controlling approach to living only makes matters worse. Control breeds contempt and frustration. Even God Himself chose not to use coercion to bring us into His will. To do so would demean human dignity, making our behavior mechanical and ultimately meaningless.

What Freedom Is

When I counsel people to set aside imperative living in favor of freedom, it is important that they get a clear picture of this concept. Freedom is not lawlessness. Within the context of freedom, we can build structure and establish boundaries—but not in a dictatorial manner. Freedom guarantees the privilege of making choices.

Two of the *Webster's Ninth New Collegiate Dictionary* definitions of *freedom* will give you an idea of what I mean:

1b. the absence of necessity, coercion, or constraint in choice or action;
1e. the quality of being frank, open, or outspoken.

My definition of freedom from imperative thinking is *recognizing the opportunity to make choices*. People who act on their ability to make choices are liberated. They are free to enjoy their closest relationships.

Freedom Puts a Priority on Relationships

When imperative thinking is traded for free thinking, personal issues switch to center stage. Performances are kept in proper perspective alongside more meaningful matters, like being loving and being understanding.

I spoke with Jack about this. "Some time ago I mentioned to you that imperative communicating sends negative messages of conditional acceptance, lack of trust, and condescension. Messages like these destroy relationships. But let's look at the positive messages accompanying freedom."

"I'm way ahead of you," Jack exclaimed. "I've already seen that when I give people freedom, they feel like I accept them and respect them. Sure enough, as soon as I see their reaction, I feel more like being flexible."

"And when you're flexible, Jack, people like Claire and your kids, for example, begin to pay more attention to what you say. In the end you feel more satisfied and secure."

Jack nodded.

Then I asked, "Can you see how freedom also causes others to feel more trusted?"

"I really can," he said. "And the neat thing is, when I show others that I trust them, they actually seem to be more trustworthy."

"Has anything happened recently that would illustrate that?" I asked.

"My daughter, Ashley, wanted to go out last weekend with some kids from church. They were going to be gone a little longer than I liked, but instead of ordering her to come home early, I told her about my concerns, then asked for her input. It kinda stunned her when I said, 'What do you think, Ashley?'"

"How was it resolved?"

"She told me she would try to stay aware of the time. And sure enough she handled it beautifully."

"So in that single incident, you showed her your acceptance and trust. And I'm assuming there was a third message—you treated your daughter as an equal."

Freedom conveys affirmation in ways an imperative statement never can. It encourages. It bolsters self-esteem. It reinforces what is good. The result is a strengthening of the bonds between the two people. Interestingly, as Jack used freedom more frequently with other people, he sensed a real change in his priorities. Performances were still important to him, but they were not all-consuming.

Liberated people can:

- allow others to be who they are.
- allow themselves to be who they are.

Allow Others to Be Who They Are

When we give freedom to others, we imply that we accept them the way they are. We recognize their privilege to have their own ideas and to express themselves in their own way. This does not mean that we must approve of everything they do. It is important to remember that we can disapprove of the act while accepting the person. For example, a family member may become very angry with me over something trivial. I don't condone this anger because I think it's a waste of emotional energy. I may even find it necessary to make it clear how much I disapprove. At the same time, I can recognize this person's freedom to be angry (even inappropriately so) and thus accept him as he is. This keeps me from making an imperative response and makes it easier to act with diplomacy and understanding.

When I shared this thought with Jack, he had a mixed response. "I can understand that I can't *make* anyone be something they're not going to be," he said. "But I'd feel like a jellyfish if I just let others rant and rave while I stood around and watched."

I smiled. "I don't think anybody would ever think of you as a jellyfish, Jack. But I want you to be able to react to situations in a way that brings you cooperation and respect in return. Remember, when we try the quick-fix (imperative) approach to our personal problems, we just muddy the waters.

"Let's take the example you mentioned a few minutes ago," I continued. "Say your fourteen-year-old daughter, Ashley, has spoken rudely to your wife. You have a choice: You can jump all over her, or you can accept the fact that she has made a mistake and talk it over with her."

Trying to consider the possibilities, Jack responded, "If I just said, 'Ashley, you look frustrated; tell me about it,' she'd be floored! Usually I start yelling in scenes like that."

"Try to imagine how your response might affect another person," I urged. "If you start yelling, Ashley will resent you. She'll either get angrier and start yelling back, or she'll swallow her feelings and let them fester inside her. Neither is a very healthy reaction."

"I see what you mean," said Jack. "I know I hid a lot of emotions when I was her age because I knew my parents or coaches would lay into me if I said anything more. But it only caused me to feel spiteful. Maybe on the outside I shaped up, but on the inside I was a time bomb."

"I'm glad you can identify with Ashley's feelings," I encouraged him. "Now let's consider what might happen if you act more accepting—if you let her know you'd like to talk to her about the way she feels, without the threat that you might humiliate her if you don't agree."

"That would be different," Jack admitted.

"It would require time and patience," I said, "but it would be worth the extra effort."

"I don't remember any time when I was allowed to express my feelings," Jack reflected. "Maybe that explains why I'm so overbearing with them now."

"Just like Ashley will be if she is forced to repress her feelings to fit your mold," I reminded him.

"So you're suggesting that I let Ashley tell me what's on her mind and that I give her some credibility?"

"That's exactly right," I said. "Keep in mind that you can still insist on good manners and a respectful attitude toward others. If discipline is necessary, it can be carried out too. But I'm suggesting that she needs to feel accepted first."

Too often we claim that we accept others for what they are when we truly mean that we accept them as long as they do what we want them to. When we truly accept others the way they are, three important by-products occur: (1) We no longer have to take unnecessary responsibility for others' emotions and behaviors, (2) we maintain emotional balance at a time when it is most needed, and (3) we encourage the other person to be more responsible for his own emotions and behaviors.

Allow Me to Be Who I Am

Freedom is not just for relationships between people. It has strong personal implications as well. Inwardly generated freedom allows me to respond to people and circumstances in the most appropriate manner. I can be genuine and open.

When I spoke with Jack about giving himself freedom to be who he is, he was not sure what to think. On one hand he said, "I've always wanted other people to accept me, so it makes sense that I'd want to accept myself." Then he hesitated. "But how can I give myself freedom to be what I am when my emotions get ugly? Are you suggesting that I'm supposed to adopt a 'hang-loose' philosophy of living?"

"Not necessarily," I replied. "What I'm suggesting is that you'll never find the balance you want by dictating to yourself. Or to put it another way, you'll only improve your emotions and relationships when your lifestyle is one of choice rather than commands."

The Choices and Consequences of Freedom

"Can you give me an example of what you're talking about?" Jack asked after I suggested his new lifestyle be made up of choices rather than imperative commands.

"Sure. Suppose you and Claire have a disagreement. As she tells you what she thinks, you have the distinct impression that she is being disrespectful. Does that ever happen?'

"Too often," he said. "I'm not saying that Claire is a hard person to live with because she's really a good woman. But sometimes I do get ticked off at the way she talks to me."

"Let's continue thinking this through," I urged him. "You begin feeling annoyed and you want to say something unkind. Right?"

"You've got me pegged." He blushed and added, "I usually snap back in a flash!"

"Okay. It's at this point that you'll want to introduce freedom to your emotions," I said.

"You mean I should just let them rip?" Jack was confused.

"No. Remember, freedom doesn't give you license for irresponsibility. It means that you have choices. When I suggest that you allow freedom to guide your thoughts, I mean that you can remind yourself that you have options. Anger is an option. Being insulting is an option. Pouting and withdrawal are options. But then, an understanding response is also an option. So is acceptance of Claire's point of view—or forgiveness of her errors. Your response does not have to be dictated by her, nor do you have to make a phony effort to follow some regulation you've heard. You are free to choose how you will respond."

Jack sat quietly for a moment, then said slowly, "I'm not sure I can process my thoughts quickly enough to consider my options. My anger seems to take hold of me and I can't stop myself."

"Sure enough, it won't be automatic as you first begin to think their way. But as freedom becomes more habitual, you'll see the common sense of it."

Self-directed freedom implies that we will do what we do because it makes sense, not because of mindless duty. For example, a husband can be pleasant to his wife, not *merely* because the Bible commands it, but because he has thought about his options and has decided to be pleasant. Or a friend can give a baby gift to her neighbor's pregnant daughter, not because she has to, but because it is what she chooses to do. A worker can obey his boss's orders, not because he's afraid of losing his job, but because he chooses to cooperate.

Realizing personal freedoms can be a refreshing experience. It highlights the fact that others cannot be held responsible for who we are. It can cause us to search for the real meaning of our convictions, and it can release us from the unhealthy clutches of others who would impose their idiosyncrasies upon us.

Being free means we are slaves to no one. And it also means we are more vigilant than ever toward our responsibilities.

The Consequences of Freedom

When we offer freedom to ourselves and to others, it does not eliminate consequences. Whether we plan it or not, each choice is followed by an effect. For example, you may allow a friend the freedom to smoke cigarettes, with the result that you spend less time together because of your distaste for smoking. You may allow a fellow employee to handle a project in his own style, with the consequence that he is responsible for any problems that may result. A wife may give herself freedom to give her husband the silent treatment for an error he made, but she should be prepared to face the repercussions of an unpleasant day.

When we use freedom sensibly—always being aware of possible consequences—we can approach problems with common sense and logic, rather than emotional outbursts.

When Jack came into my office after several weeks of replacing his imperative thoughts with thoughts of freedom, he was beaming. He told me, "I'm noticing a lot less tension in my family life. When my kids act up, rather than jumping all over them and telling them what I want them to do, I've started talking with them about choices. I know I have the option to yell, but I'm choosing to speak calmly and rationally instead. They actually listen better when I'm not so bossy. It really is making a difference."

"I'm assuming you haven't abandoned your convictions of right and wrong," I said.

"You know me better than that. But I've decided that I can tell the kids my preferences, explain all the possible consequences, then let them decide where to take things from there."

Jack was learning, as many former imperative people do, that many matters are not important enough to warrant firm reactions. And even in matters requiring a principled response, he can still communicate logically. He was learning that instead of relying on brute strength to get his ideas across, he could tell people what he thought, then let them make their own choices—and live with the consequences.

Freedom Results in Influence Without Control

Imperative people are guaranteed to be frustrated because they are chasing that impossible goal, control. While some people succeed for a time in controlling others, it is not humanly possible to control others (or even themselves) at all times.

Those who live a free lifestyle recognize this. They realize they are limited and settle on a more realistic philosophy that implies that they can have an important role in others' lives, but not the ultimate say.

Jack admitted that his old imperative patterns had drawn out nothing but imperative reactions from Claire. She had become irritable and sharp-tongued. But Jack reported that as his emotions stabilized throughout the counseling process, she responded in kind.

Shaking his head, Jack said, "Isn't it strange? By trying to force her to agree with me, I almost lost her." Then he smiled. "Now that I'm easing up on my commands, she listens to me like she cares what I think. And there are other things. Since I've been trying to have more patience, Claire has, too. The other night we really had a discussion instead of an argument. We were talking about how much allowance our kids should get and whether or not they should be expected to do certain things around the house in return. In the old days, we would have been at each other's throats, but the night before last we not only talked it over calmly, but we really *heard* each other." He grinned. "Then we got to talking about how it was when we were kids. Before you knew it, we were making popcorn and laughing like we *were* kids." Jack hesitated, and I sensed that he had something more personal on his mind.

"It's more than what we say to each other, Les. It's the way we say it. Our house had become a battleground, and our voices were like bullets. Now when Claire says my name, it's almost as if she's saying 'I love you.' That's something that hasn't happened for a long time."

Like other counselees with similar reasons for seeking help, Jack had learned that he could only have the kinds of relationships he really wanted after he got his personal house in order and learned to balance freedom with responsibility.

CHAPTER 9

Choosing to Walk Humbly

The casual observer might assume that Susan, the anxiety-ridden mother of two, currently in her second marriage, was "all together," as we say. Certainly Susan was a good actress, as most imperative people are, but her many emotional tensions told me differently.

In our sessions Susan had gained insight into her tendency to overcome inferiority feelings by maintaining a veneer of perfection. And she had grasped the idea that her imperative tendencies were at the root of her problems. She had even recognized her opportunity to make choices and had decided to choose freedom. Now she needed to allow that choice to influence her imperative personality: to replace imperative pride with humility. I suggested this to her at her next session.

After thinking for a moment, she said, "Frankly, I'm a little confused. You probably see something in me that I don't see. I'm willing to be open-minded about it, but I always thought humility was something people with puffed-up egos could use a little more of."

"No doubt about it. Arrogant people could do with a good dose of humility," I agreed. "But it's a much more complicated quality than you might think. My reason for bringing it up is that there seems to be a lot of self-preoccupied thinking at the core of your anxiety. You're putting so much emphasis on what *you* want that pride has taken a foothold."

"I *have* noticed that I'm more relaxed when I practice just being myself. But I'm curious to know how humility ties into all this."

"Think of the times when your tensions are at their peak," I urged, "whether it's when your children are giving you a bad time or when your friends aren't taking you seriously. Isn't that when your focus is on yourself? In your mind you're thinking, *How can they treat me this way? Don't they know who I am?* Your anxiety is triggered because you want the red carpet treatment and you're not getting it."

"That describes me all right. I know what I want and when I want it. I really do feel slighted when others don't respond the way I expect them to."

"I know how your mind works in those situations because that's the way I think, too," I admitted. "It's human nature to be concerned with ourselves. But that's when that old imperative thinking pops in and tries to take over. If we can stop our selfish thoughts, we can stop our imperative tendencies."

Choose to Walk Humbly

Imperative people rarely realize that they are overwhelmed by their own importance. Yet they can choose humility.

The Old Testament prophet Micah lived in a treacherous time, the reign of the wicked King Ahaz, whose imperative living ran amuck and influenced the entire

FIVE BENEFITS OF HUMBLE THINKING

1. "I don't have to fight to be best."

2. "I don't always have to be right or do things perfectly."

3. "I'm not shocked by problems, so I'm able to keep going despite them."

4. "I don't feel threatened by ideas that are different from mine."

5. "I enjoy helping others because I'm not driven to do more than I am able to do."

nation to turn away from God. Micah predicted the many disastrous results of this living in the short book of the Bible that bears his name. The city of Samaria will be reduced to a heap of ruins, he said, as will Gath, and Shaphir—the list went on and on.

Then Micah asked, "How can we come before our God now that we've committed all these sins?

"Will burnt offerings, the usual sacrifice, atone for our sins? Will thousands of rams be enough?" he asked.

"We are so desperate," he suggested, "that we will sacrifice our firstborn child if that will save us. Yet none of these extravagant offerings is enough," he said.

His final answer to that rhetorical question was simple, and yet oh so difficult.

> And what does the Lord require of you
> But to do justly,
> To love mercy,
> And to walk humbly with your God?[1]

If the people will turn from their evil ways and humble themselves, Micah promised,

> He will again have compassion on us,
> And . . . will cast all our sins
> Into the depths of the sea.[2]

We too can choose to walk humbly with our God and the people around us. *Webster's Ninth New Collegiate Dictionary* first defines the word *humble* in the negative, rather than the positive:

1. not proud or haughty: not arrogant or assertive.

Then it goes on to give a positive definition:

2. reflecting, expressing, or offered in a spirit of defer-
ence or submission.

We need to turn our proud, imperative attitudes to
attitudes that reflect submission. Yet the idea of submission is so foreign to most of us that we see humility as
weakness. It implies a wishy-washy nature, just begging
to be dominated, or a lack of character or firmness.
What a mistaken notion!

I define humility as *choosing to acknowledge our per-*
sonal limitations and choosing to be guided by a modest
sense of self-importance. Since it is the opposite of controlling behavior, humility and freedom go hand in
hand.

Susan reacted to my suggestion that she adopt a humble attitude in that same way most of my patients do:
"But what will happen? Won't other people walk all over
me?"

Humility Is Not Always a Two-way Street

A person once remarked to me that the more he understood humility, the more he realized how difficult it
was to achieve. "To be humble," he said, "means we will
go back to the way life was before sin entered the
world." He was right on target.

Prior to the Fall, God had given Adam and Eve a two-
fold plan for successful living: In essence, He said,
(1) "You have the gift of freedom" and (2) "You are to
balance this freedom by submission to My commands."
This means acquiescing to God. Humility was part of
our status from the beginning of time.

But after the Fall, Adam and Eve became uncomfort-
ably aware that trust was lost and fear had entered
men's hearts. There is no indication that they ceased be-

lieving in the ways of the Lord. If anything, they must have been more convinced than ever that God's original game plan was good. But the lost trust posed a question: If I return to the lifestyle of complete humility, how can I know I won't be dominated?

This is a valid question. In other words, I can choose to let go of my selfish, controlling habits, but there is no guarantee others will follow suit. Susan brought up this problem during our next discussion.

"First of all, I want to tell you that I've been thinking a lot about humility, Les. It seems to me that it is at the core of every lesson on living in the Bible. If I choose to be patient or kind or encouraging or forgiving, each one of these qualities means setting aside selfish demands. I really want to develop this spirit in myself, but I have one major problem. My mother lives near me, and even though I've been on my own for almost thirty years, she still hovers over me as if I were a helpless child. Whenever I let down my guard, she's ready to pounce!"

"In other words, if you are less dogmatic and more humble, you're afraid your mother might see her chance and become more bossy."

"That's exactly what would happen!"

"Let's be careful about this," I cautioned. "I think you'll agree that you don't want to start controlling again, even if your mother is bossy. The key is to learn how to be humble without letting yourself get squashed."

"Is that really possible? My mother can be pretty overbearing and I've learned that I have to be blunt with her or she walks all over me."

Susan's dilemma was common to many people who opt for the freedom of humility. When backed against a wall, it would be easy—and natural—to revert to old habits of imperative living. It all hinged on her willingness to monitor her thoughts and change her behavior accordingly.

Three Steps to Change Your Thinking

I explained to Susan that there were certain steps she could take to help restructure her thoughts.

Step #1: Identify the Moments When Self-centered Thinking Is Gaining a Foothold

"The best way to recognize faulty thinking," I told her, "is to be aware of unwanted emotions like worry, anger, resentment, or fear. These emotions are usually clear signs that you're beginning to be involved in prideful, imperative thinking."

"On the surface, that sounds pretty easy," she said, "but I'm often caught up in worry or insecurity without even being aware of it."

"Try thinking of your negative feelings as warning signals, as though a red light goes on in your mind blinking: *Slow down! Stop!* At that point you need to step back long enough to admit that you're heading for trouble. You have to be honest enough to tell yourself: *I've made a mistake. I'm creating a problem for myself.*

Step #2: Identify a Suitable Thought Alternative

"This is where we can all seek insight to make a creative choice," I told Susan. "It's all well and good to catch ourselves in the process of prideful thinking, but it doesn't mean a thing if we don't give ourselves any better alternative."

Susan looked doubtful. "I wonder if I have enough discipline for this," she said.

"It just sounds hard, Susan, because it's all new to you. Let's set up a hypothetical situation to help you. For example, imagine that you have a busy schedule planned for Monday—a meeting at the church, groceries to buy, a dentist appointment in the afternoon, and company coming for dinner. At church you are named chairperson of a committee you don't want to serve on; the bag boy at the grocery store dumps the heavy canned goods on top of your fresh peaches; the dentist says you need a root canal, and you come home with a headache as well as a toothache; and your dinner guests have a flat tire and are late for dinner, which isn't much good anyway because it has been in the oven too long.

"If my guess is right, your anxieties are in high gear. You're thinking critical thoughts about yourself, your church, the grocery store, the dentist, and your friends. Just for good measure, you blow up at your children and snap at your husband."

Susan gave me a rueful smile. "That's not a hypothetical situation, Les. I'm afraid it's pretty true to life."

"Not a pretty scene, is it? But somewhere along the way, you could have been feeling a lot better if you had caught those imperative thoughts of yours and dumped them in favor of some suitable alternatives. Can you think of any?"

Her brow wrinkled, she replied, "I guess I could have told myself that it's foolish to expect every minute of my day to go as planned. I could have been flattered by the committee's faith in me and still politely declined. I could have told my guests all about my day, and we could have had a good laugh." She sat quietly a moment, thinking. "Les, I guess it all comes down to realizing that I'm not the center of the universe and I can't expect everybody to plan their lives around mine."

"Good for you," I told her. "You're getting the idea. Now let's see if you can apply this approach to your relationship with your mother. Can you think of a recent example of her bossiness?"

"That's not hard at all," Susan said ruefully. "The other day I stopped by to see her. I was wearing a new blue dress that I thought was becoming. I was hardly in her house before she started in on me. 'I don't know why you never wear anything yellow,' she said. 'Yellow has always been so attractive on you, and that blue makes you look tired.'

"Les, I never could wear yellow. It makes me look sick. And I *know* blue is my best color. People are always telling me so. It was such a little thing, but it made me mad. I was still seething when I got home, so of course I wasn't very nice to Raymond or the children."

"Okay, Susan, now let's think about your thought alternatives."

She smiled. "It's really not so hard to figure out, is it? I could have reminded myself that yellow is my mother's favorite color, so of course she would like to see it on her daughter. I could have been flattered that she cared about what I wore. Then I could have just thought to myself, *Well, that's my mother! I can accept her and love her, but I don't have to do what she tells me to do.* I think then I would have felt relieved instead of angry."

Step #3: Choose Behaviors That Will Match Your New Thinking

"Once you're successful in confronting your thoughts," I explained, "you can then redirect your behavior. Otherwise you'll just be spinning your wheels."

"Changing my behavior is going to be the hardest thing for me to do," Susan sighed. "I hardly know where to start."

"Let's work out a practical illustration," I urged. "Can you think of a common, everyday situation at your house that might call for some redirection?"

Susan nodded. "Sometimes my husband takes forever to answer me when I ask him about our budget. He's a very methodical man and doesn't speak off the cuff. I know this, but I get impatient just the same. Before I know it, I'm trying to force an answer out of him."

"That's where you can start with Step #1. Your impatience is your red light, signaling that controlling thoughts have kicked into gear."

"Right. Then I can remind myself that I have no business picking at him and trying to get him to act the way I want him to. Step #2 would cause me to choose patience over insistence. Then I would move into Step #3 and think about better behavior." She smiled, and I could see that she was really getting into this exercise.

"Go on," I urged her.

"Well, I could tell myself to keep quiet and let him answer me in his own way. I wouldn't interrupt him as he spoke. I'd hear him out." Susan sat back in her chair and seemed to relax. "You know," she said, "I feel better already, and I have only been *talking* about what to do. The next time my mother starts telling me about how I should lose five pounds or visit her more or tell the kids not to watch so much TV, I think I'll be able to remind myself that she has a right to her opinion. I can choose to be patient, and I can look for a chance to change the subject rather than just sitting there and arguing with her."

Susan was understanding that she had the capacity to

live in humility—and that this meant strength, not weakness. Susan would benefit from a humble attitude.

Five Benefits of a Humble Attitude

A humble attitude, which acknowledges our personal limitations and is only modestly concerned with our personal importance, will change our imperative thinking to liberated thinking. We will be free to relax in the passenger's seat, rather than always having to be in control, because we will be guided by five new thoughts:

1. *"I Don't Have to Fight to Be the Best."*

In some respects it is good to be competitive. We all need to know the distinction between good, better, and best. Unfortunately, when we attempt to gain a competitive edge, it is often at someone else's expense. When comparisons become more important than relationships, we begin to look upon other people as potential adversaries. Our defenses rise; anger and resentment boil over.

On the other hand, when we embrace the spirit of humility, we can still strive for excellence, but not at the price of harmonious relationships. We can remind ourselves that we are all created equal. We can put aside our old habits of one-upmanship.

I spoke with Susan about the freedom that results when we minimize competition. "When you're feeling anxious, Susan, you may not consciously think about it, but you're worried about gaining an edge on someone. For example, let's say your mother has been giving you unsolicited advice about how you should spend your vacation time. Every time she brings up the subject, you get a knot in your stomach. Her insistent ways make you feel agitated, and you worry about how you can go ahead and do what you want to do."

Susan nodded readily. "I can think of time after time when it's happened exactly like that. I never knew how to react to her bossy ways, so I got all tensed up."

"No wonder," I replied. "Your mother was trying to prove how much better her ideas were than yours. And your anxiety showed that you wished you could prove her wrong . . . but you couldn't. Now, what do you think would happen if you just let her win? If you just do what you know is right and let her say what she likes. Above all, you don't have to try to defend yourself."

Susan was trying to make sense of my suggestion, but she looked as if she had some doubts. "You mean I can do what I will and not worry a snip about her reaction?"

"That's right," I replied. "I'm not suggesting that you should become uncaring. Certainly you'll want to treat your mother with respect. But I am suggesting that if she wants to get into a battle, you aren't obligated to fight. This is what I meant when I suggested earlier that you change your imperative thoughts, then redirect your behavior."

"I've been battling with her domineering ways all my life," Susan remarked. "It seems silly to admit, but it never dawned on me that I could simply excuse myself from the competition. What a relief that would be!"

By avoiding competitiveness in communications, Susan actually gained in several other ways:

- Her emotions remained stable because she was not caught up in her mother's emotional outbursts.
- She did not participate in the build-up of a power play, since she refrained from entering into an argument.

- She proceeded with her own decisions without getting sidetracked by fruitless discussions with her mother.
- Susan's own self-respect was communicated not in hot words but through assertive behavior.

2. *"I Don't Always Have to Be Right or to Do Things Perfectly."*

Even though I may want to share my ups and downs with someone near me, experience has taught me that I had better be judicious in how much I tell. Some people cannot be trusted to be discreet—or even to understand where I'm coming from.

It is a fact, however, that when we adopt a humble attitude, our need to defend ourselves diminishes significantly. We will still use discretion, yet we won't feel that we have to keep others at arm's length. The very act of admitting our flaws gives us a variety of freedoms:

- We needn't spend energy excusing our shortcomings because we have already admitted them.
- We can assume permission to be human.
- We no longer have to hide our mistakes.
- We can listen to criticism with an open mind.
- We can ask for help when we need it.

I had suggested in one session with Susan that she didn't need to expend so much energy defending herself.

Two weeks later she was beaming. "A couple of days ago, my husband, Raymond, was in a grouchy mood. Nothing I did seemed to please him. When I asked why he was so irritable, he just snapped that it wouldn't do any good to talk with me because I wouldn't understand anyway."

"From the way you're describing the scene, you were willing to be a comfort, but Raymond was determined to be in a bad mood."

"He sure was. Normally I would have gotten in a huff and probably would have said something like, 'Well, excuse me for living. I was only trying to help.' You know, defensive stuff like that. But I remembered what you said: 'Why defend what needs no defense?' So I just left him alone and went on about my business."

"In other words, you had a choice to make at that point and you chose not to share his tension. What happened then?"

Susan smiled. "The next morning he apologized for his bad mood, and then he thanked me for being understanding. I was floored! You know, Les, if I had become defensive and blurted out a lot of poor-me rubbish, we'd still be mad at each other. But I didn't swallow the bait on his hook."

Susan was truly free. She had admitted to herself that her marriage would not always be perfect, yet she could live with imperfection. So when an attack was unnecessarily leveled against her, she chose to stay out of the fight. Her humility allowed her to choose calmness over anger. She felt confident that she didn't have to fend off Raymond's moodiness. Though she had been given an "invitation" to become imperative, she gave herself the freedom to respond in the way she felt was right.

3. *"I'm Not Shocked by Problems, So I'm Able to Keep Going Despite Them."*

Humble people realize that problems do occur, even in the best of situations. We are willing to accept the facts and go on from there. For example, when a parent learns his child has stolen a bag of marbles from a local store, he doesn't say, "I can't believe this could happen in my family." Instead, he takes the child to the store and sees that he pays the consequences for his action. He knows things like this can happen in any family, and he realizes that choices—right ones and wrong ones—involve consequences.

Among all the issues we discussed, the idea of a "no-shock response" caught Susan's attention most powerfully. "Until you mentioned it," she said, "I would never have thought of myself as easily shocked. But now I see that throughout my adult life I've reacted to problems with disbelief. Then I immediately grew anxious and tried to take control."

"Can you think of some examples?" I asked.

"Mostly they are simple things," she replied. "For instance, I've been too easily offended when Raymond isn't interested in the same things I care about. Or I can't believe it when a friend fails to follow through on a promise."

Following her train of thought, I responded, "So whenever you didn't get your way, your imperative thoughts took over—thoughts like 'He should have . . .' or 'Why can't she just . . .'"

"I did that all the time," Susan said. "But you've helped me understand that I'm living in a dream world when I think this way. I really want to learn to see things the way they are."

"That's where humility comes in," I said. "It takes humility to acknowledge that your family is flawed or that your friends sometimes don't come through for you. Your prideful side doesn't like to admit that these things happen, even when they're obviously true."

Like Susan, we all have choices in our response to imperfection. We can pridefully presume that we should be immune to problems, thus adopting a controlling response to them. Or we can live humbly with them.

4. *"I Don't Feel Threatened by Ideas That Are Different from Mine."*

People who are humble realize that being created equal does not mean being created the same. They are open to the exciting variety that comes from different opinions, different ambitions, different lifestyles. They seek harmony rather than sameness.

Because I knew Susan's anxiety had, in part, been sparked by her efforts to maintain a cohesive family, I asked, "What situations have you encountered that have made you realize the need to find harmony in the midst of differences?"

"As I mentioned before," she said, "Raymond's son and daughter are both in their twenties, living away from home, but nearby, so we see them often. His daughter is married and has a two-year-old girl. The potential problem comes from our different styles of parenting. I've always been strict with my children, but Raymond is pretty easygoing, and his children reflect this even now."

"Are you saying your stepdaughter is a different type of mother from you—more laid back, perhaps?"

"That's an understatement. Her child is as precious as she can be, but when they come to the house I'm on pins and needles. Margaret lets the girl do a lot of things I'd never have let my children do."

Realizing that this was a good example of how Susan could learn to be tolerant rather than coercive, I asked, "How can you remain true to your convictions at a time like that without causing a rift between you and your stepdaughter?"

"It's not easy," she confessed. "Sometimes I've wanted

to let Margaret know how I feel in no uncertain terms. Other times I hover over every move the child makes. But recently I'm convinced that Margaret and I need to talk things over and see if we can develop some sort of mutual respect for each other's ideas."

"That would require a lot of self-restraint," I said.

"One thing I've learned in counseling," she offered, "is that I can choose to give a little—sometimes more than a little."

"If you can cling to that idea, Susan, it will be profitable for you. You'll be able to state your convictions tactfully and accept hers gracefully."

5. *"I Enjoy Helping Others Because I'm Not Driven to Do More Than I Am Able to Do."*

Humility does not require us to ignore our personal needs, but it gives high priority to the needs of others. The result is that we are not duty driven. Instead we help other people because we want to—and have the time to do so.

In one session, a look of quiet reflection came over Susan's face. I sat silently, knowing she needed a few minutes to put her thoughts together. Finally, she confided, "There is one thing I keep thinking about over and over." She looked intently at me. "When I'm thinking imperatively, I'm really not concerned with the needs or feelings of others. Les, I want that to change."

"Susan," I said, "I suspect that most people who know you would say that you have always been committed to your family and friends. Are you telling me now that you're ready for a new kind of commitment?"

"I really think I am," she said. "I'm beginning to understand that there's a big difference between being driven by duty and being truly committed to other people. When I'm committed to someone, like Raymond or my kids, it means I'll be looking for ways to encourage them. When I'm just doing my duty, my energy is spent trying to make them see how wonderful I am."

"So in other words, you've performed services in the past because you had to or because you wanted attention, not because you wanted to."

"I'm afraid that's right," she said. "But things are going to be different."

"Can you tell me how?"

"Well," she replied, "I'll probably continue to do most of the outward things that I've always done. What I'm aiming for are more subtle changes. When I do routine chores, I'll remind myself I'm doing them because I want our family to enjoy a well-ordered household. Instead of worrying if I'm pleasing my friends, I'll just *be* a friend."

Susan had put a lot of thought into the motivation for her new approach to living. She still wanted to maintain order in her life, but not at the high cost of emotional tension and poor relationships. Paradoxically, as she began to think more about others, she became much happier with herself, and her own emotions stabilized. It was rewarding for me to be a participant in Susan's metamorphosis. She had left the cocoon that had wrapped her tightly in anxiety and control-oriented thinking and was emerging now into a new life of freedom and humility.

pressures to face, a few bumps in the road, but I wasn't prepared for so many!"

I nodded in sympathy. It was natural for Will to feel uneasy and insecure when he had financial problems that wouldn't seem to go away. "By the end of each day," he told me, "I'm nothing but a bundle of nerves. I keep telling myself I'll be able to find some relief at home, but instead of walking into a quiet retreat, I'm swallowed up by a three-ring circus."

No wonder Will's emotions were on overload.

"What bothers me most," he admitted, "is that I'm not the friendly person I used to be. When I was in college, I was Mr. Easygoing, but now my wife says I have a sour disposition."

I had immediately sensed that Will's tension was closely linked to his need to be in control. Much of his feeling of pleasure in the past was possible because he had indeed been in control of his world. His dad had taught him to take second place to no one. He had pushed himself to excel in school and social activities. As long as he was in an academic environment, he had been able to stay on top. But that all changed when he stepped out of the ivory tower into the real world.

In one of our early sessions, I said, "Will, it seems to me that you've allowed yourself to be seduced by the idea that you should be in charge at all times. You want to make life unfold according to your directions. When this doesn't happen, you get frustrated, tense, nervous, and irritable."

Will nodded. "You know, I've been thinking along those same lines. I've been trying to figure out why I used to feel so confident, and I guess it's because everything was always going my way. I've been kicking around the idea, though, that if a person is *really* confi-

CHAPTER 10

Choosing to Be Content

People often ask me if I get tired of listening to other people's problems. They don't realize the joy that comes from participating in someone else's growth. It makes me feel great when I see people making major changes in their lives. I have learned that many people have the capability to be free. They have just been looking for someone to offer a jump-start.

One such person was Will. A dentist in his early thirties, Will had sought counseling because of tremendous stress. He reported being unusually irritable both at work and at home. While he once had dreamed of financial freedom, he now felt burdened by the huge debt acquired when he opened his practice. He told me his marriage was not exactly breaking up, but it wasn't very rewarding either. He loved his three children—ages seven, four, and two months—but sometimes life with them seemed overwhelming.

Will told me in our first session, "I had always dreamed of a happy adult life. Sure, I knew I'd have dent, he can stay with his personal game plan even when life isn't agreeable."

"I like what you're saying," I told him. "Someone else said something like it a long time ago." Then I encouraged Will to reread some of Paul's words in the book of Philippians: "I have learned the secret of being content in any and every situation, whether well fed or hungry, whether living in plenty or in want. I can do everything through him who gives me strength."[1] The apostle Paul chose to be content in whatever situation he was in.

"That's the kind of game plan I'm talking about," Will agreed. I've always wanted to be calm and sure of myself. But I'm going through a real struggle to get my business off the ground, and I can't say I feel very secure financially. Yet the kind of contentment Paul is talking about doesn't depend on monthly statements, does it?"

As the weeks passed, Will was able to target several personal areas that needed improvement. For example, he made up his mind to be pleasant to his staff even when work was difficult and he was under pressure. It wasn't their fault, he reasoned, that he was having financial problems. Likewise, he knew he would need to temper his authority at home with kindness, understanding, and good humor. He told me, "Twenty years from now I don't want my kids to remember me as nothing but an old grouch."

Curious about his motives, I said, "Will, I know you're really determined to make changes in your behavior, and I applaud that. But how about your feelings? How can you know that you're not just repressing those angry emotions that started your problems?"

"I figured you'd ask me something like that, and I'm ready for you, Les. I'm trying to let awareness be my guide. I'm *aware* when I'm tempted to let my irritability take over. As soon as I'm aware, I remind myself that I have a choice. I don't *have* to fly off the handle. Losing my cool has become a bad habit, but habits can be broken. Also, I'm realizing more and more that control isn't always a good thing. I'll control what I can and should. But when I can't, I'll admit my limitations and let matters rest."

Once we embrace liberated thinking as a way of life, we will choose to treat people differently.

We Will Choose to Respect Other People

When people like Will are driven by imperative commands, they become so focused on everyday problem solving that they see the people around them as a means to an end, robots whose function is to "do the job right." In contrast, people who are free from the demands of imperative living can continue to be involved in their daily responsibilities without overlooking others. Their concern for others communicates respect.

Will spoke with me about this issue. "Les, I've noticed that when my mind is focused entirely on the job at hand, my mood changes completely. I become abrupt and short tempered."

I knew exactly how he felt. "It's so easy to get caught up in tunnel vision that we forget that these are *people* we're working with—people who have sensitivities, needs, and emotions of their own," I told him.

"I've decided that I never want to be so intent on what I'm doing that I lose touch with people," Will said. "It isn't any sacrifice for me to be polite or listen. I guess I'm saying that no task should be so all-important that it keeps me from respecting the people I'm working with—or the people I go home to after work!"

"It will be a major step forward if you can be consistent with this kind of behavior," I said. "Are you up to it?"

Will nodded. "But there are just two problems that I need to get a handle on. First, it's a little hard to show respect when I think someone is doing a lousy job. And second, it's hard to take time for people when my busy schedule gets me up against the wall."

"Let's talk about some behavior habits you can cultivate that won't be dislodged by pressure, someone else's imperfections, or poor job performance."

Will and I then discussed how he could clearly communicate respect, even in difficult situations.

(1) He would take time at the beginning of each day, then two or three times throughout the day, to speak to his employees about something in their personal lives. For example, he might ask his secretary how she enjoyed her daughter's soccer game the evening before. Or he might tell her about an upcoming TV program that her ten-year-old son would like. Or he might even ask her if her headache is better. This kind of conversation would remind him that he was dealing with a person with a life of her own outside the office.

(2) Even when pressed by a heavy schedule, he would take time to listen to an employee's suggestions. And he would return phone calls promptly. This would remind him that it was important to think about somebody besides himself.

(3) He would allow his coworkers the privilege of completing tasks their own way, rather than insisting they do it his way. This attitude would remind him to respect other people's skills.

(4) When his employees made mistakes, he would encourage them to see these as learning experiences. This would remind him that other people make errors (which also allowed him to make a few).

We Will Choose to Empathize With Other People

Empathy is more than understanding or concern. To emphathize, it is necessary to *feel with* another person. I suggested that Will might get a better idea of what empathy is all about by thinking about how someone else is feeling in a given situation. I told him to choose anyone he liked, then imagine how it must be to walk in that person's shoes. This would require a lot of imagination and some creative thinking, but I felt confident Will could do it.

The next week he told me about an incident with a close friend. "My friend Gary came into the office with a broken filling. He began telling me about a major setback with his job. He had been expecting a promotion, but his boss dropped a bomb instead. The company was going to have layoffs, and Gary's job would be on the line.

"As he was telling me the details, I thought about our conversation about empathy. Normally, I would have given him some quick advice and hurried along. Even though I had a full schedule, I decided to sit down with him for a few minutes. 'This is really tough,' I told him. 'I can imagine what a blow it must have been, especially when you were expecting good news. It's enough to shake a guy up.'"

"How did Gary respond?"

"At first he just sat there and looked at me. Then he started to tell me how helpless losing his job made him feel, how it was going to affect his whole family. Once he got started, he couldn't seem to stop. It was as if he had been waiting for someone who cared enough to sit down and listen. I'll tell you the truth, Les, I didn't have to pretend I cared. I really did!"

"Will, I think you're seeing the difference between your old habit of handing out pat answers and this new style of understanding. Taking the time to empathize can be an exciting experience."

"You said it. When I used to try to tie up every problem into a neat package, it only made me more tense. It didn't do much for the people around me, either. I've had to realize that some matters can't be laid to rest as easily as that. Besides when I gave people pat answers, it probably sounded as if I didn't really care."

Empathy recognizes that sharing can be far more important than giving advice or doing favors. Because of our natural tendency to impose our own opinions and feelings on others, empathy is not always a natural response. Yet when we take the emphasis away from self and shift attention to the other person, it can become an integral and rewarding part of our relationships.

Neither respect nor empathy mean that we are not firm with members of our family or our employees or our friends.

We Will Choose to Be Firm Without Being Overpowering

Sometimes it is necessary to draw definite boundaries of discipline and principle. For example, parents do their children no favors if they exercise no discipline. Spouses and friends do each other no service if they hold to no principles of right and wrong. The key to balancing humility and firmness is knowing how to be firm without being overbearing.

Firmness is likely to be out of bounds when it is accompanied by the following traits:

- Sarcasm or cynicism
- Annoyance that lingers long after the cause

- Accusing questions such as, "Why do you always have to . . . ?" or "What makes you think you can . . . ?"
- Overwhelming explanations of your convictions
- A coercive tone of voice.

Many imperative people find balanced firmness most difficult in the small issues of life. They can be so exact in their expectations that they hold grudges that hardly matter. An awareness of this tendency caused Will to make his greatest changes. He had told me how his tensions were aggravated by his wife's insensitivities—that's what he called her reactions when they weren't the same as his.

"Look, Will, you'll be doing both yourself and your wife a favor if you can just say what you think about something without laundering it and hanging it out to dry. You have some good ideas, but nobody is going to be willing to listen if you're overbearing."

Will nodded. "I know I come on pretty strong, but once I get started, it sure is hard to stop. I've always thought that anything less than full persuasion was wishy-washy. But I'll have to admit that I'm miserable when I keep on and on about something without seeing any results."

"What about the people who have to listen to you? Don't you suppose they feel miserable too?"

Will agreed to make a list of the issues he had tried to control too firmly. Many of the things he mentioned were everyday problems. He insisted on a clean house, with everything dusted and polished according to his directions. He wanted his wife to use a particular tone of voice when she spoke to him about a problem. He expected her to be understanding about his work, even when she was exhausted from a hard day at home. He demanded that she discipline the children just as he would.

When Will took a good look at his list, he shook his head. "These are finicky problems," he admitted. "From now on I'm going to speak firmly about issues that really matter to me and try to keep normal differences in perspective."

Will's experience illustrates that changes can definitely be made when there is a commitment to humility. He was coming to realize that he could still speak forcefully when necessary, but without endangering personal relationships.

People have often asked me if they have the right to express anger and frustration. My answer is that I'm not as interested in rights as responsibilities. In other words, is it *responsible* to express anger and frustration? Ask yourself this question the next time you feel like flying off the handle. Can you, like Will, choose to say what you think without being overpowering?

We Will Choose to Be Honest

In working with Will, it became apparent that he had spent a lot of time trying to make it appear as if he didn't have any problems—a sure path to heavy strain on the emotions.

"Will," I asked, "wouldn't you feel a lot less pressure if you could just let people see the real you, lumps and all?"

A blank look came over his face. "I've never even considered the possibility of letting my weaknesses all hang out. My problems aren't anybody else's business."

"So you work like a Trojan trying to keep up the pretense, and in the meantime you feel miserable and your relationships are coming unhinged."

He shook his head. "I'd be scared to death to let down

my guard. I don't know what people would think if I let them see the real me."

"It's unsettling, isn't it? After all, there isn't any guarantee that others will accept you if you turn out to be a mere mortal."

He chuckled, but I thought he looked a little uncomfortable.

"Will, none of us is free of problems, but we can't afford to let ourselves get caught up in the game of pretense. It leads nowhere. Let me challenge you to have the courage to let people see your weaknesses as well as your strengths."

When Will returned for his next appointment, he had a look of relief on his face. "What have you been up to?" I asked.

"That challenge of yours really got to me," he admitted. "I started paying closer attention to how I act around other people. For example, my wife asked me about my day last Friday, and I noticed that I couldn't bring myself to tell her I had to meet with my banker about restructuring my loan."

"What kept you from being honest with her?"

"I was afraid she'd be disappointed in me," he said. "After I realized that I couldn't talk with her about this, I began thinking that I must have been this way for years. I've been a phony for so long that pretense is a way of life. If I keep on like this, we won't have any relationship at all."

"You've really been putting a lot of energy into covering up," I told him. "And you've tried to hide the way you feel about not being perfect. No wonder you're tense."

"But that's going to change," he declared. "I sat down with my wife and told her about our financial problems. I even told her how scared it made me feel not to be on top of things. And do you know what she did? She thanked me for being open and honest with her. Can you beat that?"

Will was discovering a new way of life. He felt freedom in an unusually large dose because he had been captive to dishonest emotions for such a long time. He needed to admit that he had human frailties, just like the rest of us.

We Choose to Seize the Initiative

Living a liberated lifestyle involves more than just choosing to treat people with respect and have empathy for their feelings. It is necessary to seize the initiative. What does this mean, and how can you learn to do it? Let me tell you about a talk I had with Will.

"I really look forward to our talks each week," he told me one day. "And I've just recently realized why. It's been a long time since I've allowed myself the luxury of letting my hair down with anyone and really sharing personal thoughts and feelings. These talks are a breath of fresh air."

"I'm encouraged for you, Will, and I'll have to tell you that I enjoy our talks too. Out of curiosity, do you ever notice that the style of our discussions has a carry-over effect in your personal life?"

"I sure do," he replied. "I've become keenly aware of how most men *and* women hesitate to talk about really personal matters. I keep remembering my experience with Gary and how he opened up to me. I'm making a point of trying to be more relaxed when I talk to people. They seem to respond better to someone who doesn't act as if he's late for an appointment.

"Also, I'm more easygoing with our three children. In the past it was a rare thing for me to laugh with them or to get down on the floor and play with them. But

I've decided that the most important thing I can teach them is to relate to other people—and that starts with me!"

"These are good examples of what I'm talking about when I say we can seize the initiative in bringing personal issues out in the open," I said. "I can see that you're beginning to talk about more than superficial matters . . . whether with your wife, your kids, or with friends."

"I'll have to admit it's a conscious effort right now," he responded, "but I hope it will become automatic. The interesting thing is, when I ask people how they feel about a wide range of subjects—anything from jogging to the latest book they've read—I realize I'm really interested in their answers. And I'm able to respond with positive comments instead of offhand remarks. I can't say I'm used to all this yet, but I can say it's getting easier."

Will and I talked about some acts of initiative that we can all use to express a more personal style of communication:

- Taking time to compliment others, explaining why you appreciate them
- Admitting a feeling of insecurity
- Disclosing a time when your plans failed
- Urging someone to tell you more about their own preferences and goals

Seizing the initiative to be personal is a type of servitude. It indicates a willingness to become involved in another person's life. It demonstrates an openness that makes others feel comfortable in drawing near. It builds bridges.

How About You?

Are you really willing to exchange your imperative thinking for liberated thinking? The statements below are common to liberated thinking. Check the ones that now reflect your attitude.

1. ____ "I keep projects in perspective—people still matter."
2. ____ "I am willing to view different ideas with an open mind."
3. ____ "I am willing to let other people pursue tasks in their own fashion."
4. ____ "I am willing to admit when I'm wrong."
5. ____ "When other people make mistakes, I won't immediately react with anger."
6. ____ "When someone has a personal problem, I will try to listen rather than immediately suggest a solution."
7. ____ "I still have strong beliefs about what is right and wrong, but I will realize that I am not all knowing."
8. ____ "When someone disappoints me, I'll take time to allow my emotions to settle before I address the problem."
9. ____ "I still have standards of excellence, but I do not use these standards as criteria for accepting or rejecting others.
10. ____ "When someone confronts me, I will realize that what they have to say is worthy of my consideration."

If you checked six of the above statements, you are beginning to change your imperative thinking to liberated thinking.

This change will benefit you, as well as your family, friends, and business associates. Two major benefits are a new, objective viewpoint, which will help you to make more logical decisions, and a feeling of joy, despite the external circumstances in which you find yourself.

Objectivity

Objectivity is the ability to observe a situation with fairness and logic, unhindered by biases or preconceived ideas. Imperative people are so tied up in their self-imposed rules of right and wrong that they feel they are somehow betraying their own commitments if they become objective.

A good example was Ethel, a very rigid woman whose religious beliefs were cast in stone. Her husband, on the other hand, had what she called "a complete lack of religious fervor." She handled the situation by constantly picking and nagging at him, then playing the martyr when he didn't respond.

"Ethel," I said, "have you ever tried to look at your husband's attitude objectively . . . to really understand the way he feels?"

"Why should I?" she shot back. "My spiritual convictions are the most important things in my life, and I'm not going to compromise them for *anyone!*"

In a technical sense, Ethel was correct to realize that her husband needed faith, as we all do. But by trying to force him into her pattern, she slammed the door on open discussion and possible spiritual growth.

It helps to remember that other people can—and indeed will—have ideas and preferences that do not necessarily make sense to us. Even so, these people are free to think as they choose. By being objective, we can accept the existence of different ideas without compromising our own convictions. We can keep communication lines open without trying to control.

The next time Will came into my office, I mentioned the need for greater objectivity.

He shook his head in mock disgust. "My entire education has been based on the scientific approach," he said. "I learned to measure the facts precisely, then respond to them accordingly. But I guess I haven't done a very good job of carrying this over into my personal life. I've had my own ideas about how things should be, and I've tried to force myself and everyone around me to fit those ideas. That doesn't seem very objective, does it?"

"It's easy to be objective when you're working with problems that are impersonal," I told him. "But it's a lot harder when your own emotions or your future well-being is at stake."

"I'm glad to hear you say that because I can tell it's going to take a lot of practice to set aside my biases when I'm dealing with problems close to home."

"Can you give me an example?"

"I sure can. Let's say that I go home this evening and my son seems distracted . . . he doesn't care about a thing I say. If I could be objective, I'd tell myself that no kid is ever going to be in a good mood all the time. But you and I know that objectivity isn't natural at times like these. My old imperative habits goad me into thinking, *That kid had better straighten up and pay attention when I talk to him.*

"That's a pretty good example," I said.

Will nodded. "I'll have to admit I didn't make it up. That kind of thing happens at my house all the time. I know how I ought to think and act, but it's easy to jump in with both feet and end up in an emotional scene. How can I keep that from happening?"

Will and I talked about ways we can all keep from reverting to control tactics in family situations. To be objective, we decided it is helpful to cling to these thoughts:

- I am limited in my ability to solve the problems of other people.
- There will never be a completely tension-free day.
- I'm not perfect, so it's only fair to let others be imperfect.
- There are no guarantees that others will care to live according to my values.

Objectivity produces flexibility, which allows us to embrace a broad spectrum of truths, both pleasant and unpleasant, rather than just clinging to those truths that please ourselves. While objectivity does not downgrade emotions, it does keep them from overwhelming us.

Joy

Joy is the ability to appreciate what is good and lasting. It is satisfaction with life.

In one of our early conversations, Will had confessed that he had little joy in his life. "I can laugh at a good joke or funny story," he had told me, "but I don't very often feel that warm inner glow."

"Will, you'll find that joy seems to elude imperative people. Even if you do succeed in dominating people or accomplishing many tasks, there is no lasting reward because the payoffs are temporary and external. Joy comes when you give others *and* yourself permission to be free. Then when something pleasurable happens, you have the extra thrill of knowing that it wasn't forced."

Later, Will beamed as he told me about a Saturday

with his seven-year-old son. "My son, Matthew, has always wanted me to take him fishing at the stock pond on my dad's property. I've gone with him a couple of times, but I never enjoyed it because I was too impatient. I'd always have to make sure Matthew did exactly as I told him. And you can guess how well that worked! But last Saturday was different. Instead of forcing him to act like an adult, I let him be a seven-year-old. And we had a ball! We only caught a couple of small fish. But that didn't matter."

"What did matter?" I asked.

"I took time to enjoy the little things. I told Matthew funny stories about when I was a kid. I let him tell me silly things about his buddies. Not once did I try to make him fit into some preconceived mold. I haven't felt that way in months, maybe years. And all I had to do was relinquish control."

"You discovered something important then, didn't you? Your day with Matthew wasn't filled with achievement. You only caught a couple of fish, and Matthew probably didn't learn to bait the hook exactly the way you did, but you found out that joy doesn't depend on perfect performance. It's an outflow of love."

Will had discovered that all his perfectly laid plans did not have to fall into place before he could relax and have a good time. He realized that there is no such thing as a problem-free life, yet joy can be experienced just the same. He was learning to find it in the blessings of every day and in the knowledge that he had much to give to the people who mattered most to him.

The final step in my counseling of imperative people is to help them apply their liberated thinking to their relationships with their spouses, their children, and God. We'll look at these relationships in Part Four of this book.

PART FOUR

Enjoying
Relationships
with
Other People

CHAPTER 11

Freedom and Marriage

When I talk with married couples about developing an atmosphere of freedom in their relationship, I receive mixed reactions. Some spouses are enthusiastic. They tell me they are tired of being fenced in, and freedom sounds like a wonderful relief. Others, fearful that their mate will be uncooperative, balk.

"That sounds like a one-way street," one woman told me. "If I give my husband complete freedom, no telling what he'll do!"

I remind these people that a marriage based on control will guarantee those very problems they fear. Marriage can thrive only when both husband and wife feel safe in their relationship. When they sense that it is okay to reveal themselves to each other without being afraid of rejection or reprisal, harmony becomes possible.

I want to repeat: harmony is possible only when we are willing to accept each other's differences.

In my discussions with Bob and Elaine (the couple introduced in chapter 1) we eventually talked about the practical implications of freedom within their marriage.

"I've known for some time," Elaine said, "that I needed to make some big changes in the way I relate to other people, and I've even tried to follow some advice that I read. But I realize now that these how-to efforts didn't do me much good because I wasn't aware of the mental adjustments I needed to make first. I've learned that I need to get my thinking in gear before I can change my behavior."

"So now you know the thought patterns that need your special attention. As you change internally, external changes can take place. Elaine, I'm very encouraged for you."

"Bob and I have been together too long to let our marriage flounder now," Elaine explained. "Before counseling, we somehow allowed ourselves to get pulled into a downward spiral of unproductive communication. But in the last couple of months our interaction has been much better. It's a relief to have positive goals to look forward to."

Bob nodded. "I've always admitted that I needed to work harder at making our marriage work, but I honestly didn't do much to change. I kept hoping I could make Elaine change instead. I didn't realize until recently that this attitude showed how much I was trying to control her."

"I'm always interested in knowing what areas you've concentrated on most as you've made adjustments," I said.

"I'm learning to accept Elaine as she is," Bob told me. "It isn't my job to make her fit my mold. That means setting aside those old ideas of getting her to do everything *my* way."

"I'm trying to make the same effort," Elaine admitted.

"I'm also learning that my controlling tendencies are directly related to my own emotional balance. The more caught up I am in worry or anger or false guilt, the more likely I am to take it out on Bob."

The willingness of Bob and Elaine to examine themselves first before focusing on each other was especially gratifying to me. Too often my counseling can be slowed down by couples who want to do little more than point accusing fingers at one another and say, "If only he (or she) would change, *then* I could live a decent life." We all agree that life with a compatible partner is desirable, yet some of us never seem to realize that we are the ones who need to work hardest on compatibility.

Once you understand the dangers of imperative living and embrace freedom as a healthier alternative, you will be free to discover how your new lifestyle affects a primary relationship like marriage. I have found that a good place to begin this process is in discussing a couple's ideas about leadership and submission, for it is here that imperative thinking may already be entrenched.

Leadership and Submission

Because of differing expectations regarding the nature of their roles, spouses can have divergent opinions about these two qualities. I have noticed that many men exhibit disturbing thoughts about a husband's leadership. Many assert, "I'm the man of this house and I'm *not* going to have some woman telling me what to do." They presume that leadership means a license to dominate. Wives exposed to such heavy-handedness respond: "I don't have to put up with this kind of treatment. I have rights, too, you know."

I do believe that men have a God-given role as leaders in the family. But let's be sure to understand what leadership is and is not. Leadership is the ability to inspire and influence others. Within the context of a family this implies that the leader guides family members toward loving relationships and responsible behavior.

At the same time, God has instructed both husbands and wives to be submissive. How can this work? Submission in marriage is the willingness of *each* spouse to join with the other in maintaining an atmosphere of love and respect.

"I've always assumed that a husband should be the leader," Bob admitted when I asked the Wrights to discuss their roles with me. "I would have thought submission was for women and wimps."

"That's a common misconception," I said. "The truth is, real leadership is impossible without an accompanying commitment to submission."

"I like the idea of submission being shared by both the husband and wife," Elaine put in. "That sounds like teamwork."

Bob nodded. "I guess it does make good sense. But what does it have to do with freedom?"

"The only way this concept of leadership and submission can work is if it is accomplished within a context of freedom," I told him. "These qualities are not obligations. They are choices. When husbands and wives *choose* to follow God's wishes, good things can happen."

Keeping Score

When emotional strains enter a marriage, it is very common for one spouse to accuse the other of not trying hard enough. "Why is it that I'm the one who always has to make all the adjustments?" is a typical complaint. When I have spoken separately with each spouse about the same problem, I've heard each one swear that the other is doing nothing constructive at all, while the person I'm talking to is working overtime to be a peace-maker.

When we begin keeping score on each other's efforts, we don't see much progress. Instead, we accuse, we co-erce, and we throw up our hands in defeat. Keeping score perpetuates imperative thinking.

When we offer freedom within marriage, we grant our mate the choice of responding to problems in what-ever way he or she deems appropriate. When the choice is a poor one, we may be disappointed, but we no longer will fall back on the old imperative habit of demanding perfection.

Elaine tried to be diplomatic about this with Bob. "Honey, there have been times when you've felt that you were the only one trying to make our marriage work. You've even accused me of letting you make all the ad-justments. I hope you can understand now that I'm really committed too. Just because I manage things dif-ferently, it doesn't mean I'm not trying."

"Sometimes you withdraw when we disagree," he told her, "and I get the feeling that you're punishing me and waiting for me to shape up. It would be better if we could keep communicating."

"I'll admit that I've used the silent treatment to make you uncomfortable," Elaine said. "I just want you to know that I'm willing to keep trying, and I hope you are too."

I interjected, "Couples often make the mistake of as-suming the marital success is a fifty-fifty proposition, but it usually doesn't work that way."

Bob looked puzzled, so I explained, "When we think in fifty-fifty terms, we're likely to say to ourselves, 'I'm doing my half, so you'd better do yours.' We get side-tracked by scorekeeping."

"What do you suggest?" Bob asked.

"What about a one hundred-zero approach? Each one of you can say, 'If this relationship is going to succeed, it's one hundred percent up to me.' This means no score will be kept on the other person's efforts."

"Don't you think that's risky?" Elaine asked. "Couldn't it lead to martyrdom?"

"It could indeed," I admitted. "But I'm not suggesting that either of you set yourselves up for martyrdom. I'm suggesting that you can each be trying so hard that you won't worry about who isn't staying even."

Setting Boundaries Without Threats

Freedom does not imply an absence of structure. America is a nation anchored in freedom, but we maintain laws for the purpose of preventing anarchy. Likewise, married couples can respect certain principles that prevent disorder. But maintaining both structure and freedom is no easy matter; it requires delicate balance in thinking and speaking.

Too many spouses make the mistake of communicating their ideas in overbearing ways, thereby making them sound like threats. Some are outspoken in their declarations; others are manipulative in subtle ways.

Both Bob and Elaine recognized the mistakes they frequently made by communicating threats. Bob was a more overbearing communicator, so his threats were easy to recognize. Elaine was more evasive; she used passive control tactics. But each was sending the same message: "You'll be sorry for what you've just said."

In one of our discussions, I mentioned an argument they had told me about. "Bob, you recently told Elaine very forcefully that she'd better stop spending so much money. And you told me that she was very stubborn in her response. How do you think you could state your feelings differently?"

"I guess I need to do less talking and stick to my guns.

We each have a certain amount of cash we spend on miscellaneous items. When Elaine spends too much, I gripe at her, but I always end up giving her extra money out of my amount."

"You mean you could stop giving her money from your fund?"

He nodded.

"I've always wondered why he rarely sticks to the rules," Elaine said. "I think we have a fair system of handling money. So if he's mad at me for my spending, fine. He can make his point by not doling out the extra cash. I can live with that. I'd just like to see an end to the power plays."

Too often we establish good principles, but we don't reinforce them with actions. Assuming that fairness is being used in setting up the structure for a marital relationship, spouses eliminate unnecessary bantering when they let their actions do the talking. Threats can be eliminated altogether. In using this approach we communicate: "You are free to handle your responsibilities as you choose; understand that I will remain firm in my convictions."

Understanding Takes Priority

The word *convince* is derived from a Latin word meaning to conquer. When we are trying to convince one another, we are attempting to overwhelm each other, to render each other powerless. This eventually causes resentment and futility.

Spouses are not meant to be adversaries. The husband-wife team is a union. Convincing communication has no part here.

When I explained this to Bob and Elaine, he spoke up. "But if I really feel strongly about something, how am I supposed to get Elaine to understand my point of view?"

"First, why not just tell her what you think without being a high-pressure salesman? I think she'll be more inclined to respect your viewpoint when you're not pushing her. Second, be sure you don't concentrate so hard on making your point that you forget to let her know you understand where she's coming from.

"One of the most powerful tools of persuasion," I told Bob, "is an understanding spirit. When Elaine feels that you are tuned in to her feelings, you won't have to force her to listen. She'll be ready and willing."

"Bob and I are great debaters," Elaine said, "but that only gets us in a tug of war. I can see that I need to work on being understanding too."

"The next time Bob offers a suggestion," I said to her, "you might try responding with an open mind. Even if you don't agree with him, let him see that you're listening to what he has to say. And remember that interrupting with "buts" could ruin this interchange. For example, don't say, 'I know you're disappointed that I forgot to take the shirts to the cleaners, but you ought to try to juggle my schedule sometime.' Just listen understandingly and leave it at that."

"Do you realize how different that would be for both of us?" Bob asked. "We can both be pretty strong-willed. What you're asking is going to take a lot of restraint."

I nodded. "I know from personal experience that it's easier to be coercive. But being understanding is consistent with the philosophy of freedom and humility. It's the only way a marriage can thrive."

Demonstrating understanding does not imply a lack of conviction. It shows that we believe others should be given attention and respect.

A Bondslave's Security

I have spoken with countless spouses who admit they stay married only because they feel compelled to. To them, marriage is a drudgery that must be endured. They may feel bound by religious pressure or they may stay together for the sake of their children. Some say they stick it out because of business and social pressures.

I deeply believe in lasting commitments to marriage. Instead our throw-away culture has encouraged lax attitudes toward marital vows. If it's not what we want, we're encouraged to toss it and look for something better. This mindset feeds self-indulgence, which in turn does little to undergird marital loyalty.

However, commitment at gunpoint is no commitment at all. It provides no marital security, and it is an unhealthy form of loyalty.

In days of Roman rule, a slave master had the prerogative of giving his slave a writ of freedom. A slave could be released from all obligations to the master. However, some slaves, upon receiving their freedom, would decide they wanted to remain with the master. An agreement would stipulate that the freed man would continue to do his former work, with the understanding that he did so out of desire rather than compulsion. He was given the title, bondslave.

So it can be in marriage. Husbands and wives know that they do not *have* to remain committed to one another. (Indeed, our divorce laws reflect this attitude all too well.) Yet they will freely choose a commitment as powerful as a bondslave's commitment to do his master's bidding. They become bondslaves to each other, free to leave, yet determined to stay and serve.

You are probably thinking, *Now wait a minute, Les. You told us back in chapter 8, "Being free means we are slaves to no one."* That is true, and I stand by my statement. What I'm saying here is that in the marriage commitment you become *as* bondslaves, not to a slave master, but to each other. You choose freely to serve, to cherish, to love.

Elaine told me privately about the choice she had made and the transformation that had occurred in her heart. "Several years ago I was very disillusioned with my marriage. I wanted out in the worst way, but our boys were in grade school and I couldn't bear putting them through a divorce. I stuck it out, but my heart wasn't in it."

"What about now?" I asked. "Are you still staying with Bob because you feel you have to?"

"Not at all. Of course our problems haven't completely gone away, and I know we may never have a perfect marriage. But the change in me has a lot to do with choice. I realize I *can* leave Bob any time I want. I'm capable of making a living on my own, and I assume our kids would survive. But the point is, I *want* to be committed to him. I *want* to be loyal."

"I'm sure you've thought about the many positive implications of this," I responded.

"Yes, I have. It means that when I put up with Bob's inconsistencies, I know I'm doing it because I love him, not because it's my duty. And when I take charge of my moods and my words in the many ways we've discussed, I'm not doing it because it's an assignment. I do it because it makes good sense."

I smiled with her. "You've found a good balance, Elaine. You are committed to freedom, which is necessary for personal composure. But you're also committed to structure, which carries you through frustrating times."

A bondslave to marriage realizes how fickle emotions can be. Romantic, "in-love" feelings are pleasant, but they can't be trusted to remain steady. Too many distractions can cause them to fade. A freely chosen "enslavement" to marriage transcends an emotional commitment. It is characterized by thought and purpose and can see beyond momentary distractions. Bond-slaves are capable of a resilient love because they have taken the time to consider consequences.

Love Is Not Based on Performance

I recall talking with a couple who very calmly stated, "We no longer love each other." Reading between the lines, I interpreted this to mean, "My spouse quit giving me what I wanted, so I withdrew my affection."

Any of us can respond warmly and affectionately when another person acts in accordance to our agenda. But love based strictly on such feel-good experiences is superficial. In fact, it may not represent love at all. In many cases, it is a self-centered satisfaction that circumstances are under control.

Free, humble spouses love because it is part of what they are, not because another has finally made the grade. Love is an extension of inner maturity rather than adolescent-like immaturity.

"I'm sure you didn't intentionally plan it this way," I told Bob, "but in the past you quietly decided that you would love Elaine only when she performed according to your specifications. That was a form of conditional acceptance."

"Yeah, but that's changing now," he declared. "When you challenged me to apply freedom to my circumstances, it hit me like a ton of bricks. I'm free to hold onto my petty anger, or I'm free to set it aside in favor of a loving response. I know that doesn't sound like a revolutionary idea to you, but it was sure something I'd never thought about before."

I nodded. "I know it's much easier to behave lovingly when your wife is doing what you expect of her. But it's also nice to know that your love for her doesn't have to be based on her latest good behavior. Love is drawn from within. It's a spiritual quality, a gift from God, and it can transcend uncomfortable circumstances."

I want to emphasize that a nonperformance-based love is uncommon to humans because of our natural inclination toward self-preoccupation. Unconditional love, on the other hand, is a commitment to let God change our self-centeredness.

Bob shared with me how he had made a major spiritual adjustment that directly affected his ability to love. "Although I've been a Christian for several years, I was still trying to control my marriage. But when I discovered I could choose to let God be in charge of our marriage, things changed."

"What do you mean?" I asked.

"I very specifically pray that God will help me set aside my need for control so I can be kind and patient even when Elaine isn't being very lovable."

"So you've made your love for her a matter of the will," I reflected, "based on your most important spiritual convictions."

"Yes, but it hasn't made me feel like I *have* to love her, and it hasn't made love boring. I think it has deepened our bond because now it's clear that I'm not going to give up on our marriage."

Bob and Elaine never did completely erase the differences and flaws in their marriage. Rather, they developed a new depth in their relationship as they learned to exchange their controlling, imperative pattern of thinking for a mindset of freedom. They had a new method of responding to the inevitable tensions marriage can bring. The result was mature emotions and a more secure future.

CHAPTER 12

Freedom and Parenting

A friendly, outgoing person, Carol was quick to say yes when friends asked for her help. She enjoyed being active, but had pushed herself to the point of burnout. When I first met her, she was worried about her mother's life in a nursing home, overextended in her children's many activities, and loaded with community obligations.

In our counseling we identified that she need not take on the burden of being everyone's hero, and Carol successfully trimmed her schedule to reflect more balanced thinking. As the sessions progressed, however, one area received an increasing amount of attention: parenting.

In our first few meetings we had discussed a couple of incidences related to her eleven-year-old daughter, Lana, and her eight-year-old son, Keith. I had suggested that it would be helpful if Carol were less dictatorial, if she would emphasize choices instead of commands. So it was no surprise when she brought up the subject of her children a few weeks later.

"I don't know if my kids are under a bad influence at school or what," she complained, "but they've been terribly unruly lately. I try to get them to mind, but I have to repeat myself six times before they listen. I'm afraid if I don't stop some of their disobedient tendencies now, their teen years will be disastrous."

"Can you give me an example of the kind of behavior you're concerned about?"

"I sure can. Our latest flap has been over the music videos they want to watch on TV. You know, rock videos. Have you seen what is allowed on the airwaves? It's pure filth!"

"I agree. Secular music has always tended to emphasize sensuality, but in the past several years it's gotten out of hand. And to make matters worse, it's visually portrayed in these videos."

"Then you'd agree with me that my eight-year-old son and eleven-year-old daughter don't need to be watching that garbage?" Carol asked.

I nodded agreement.

"I've already forbidden the music videos on our own TV," she explained, "but I've learned that Lana and Keith watch it when they are in their friends' homes. I'm determined to put a stop to this."

"Have you talked with your kids about it?"

"You bet I have. I told them that if a friend turns on the music channel, they are to come home."

While I was in agreement with Carol's principles, I was concerned about her heavy-handed tactics. She had not talked *with* her children, as she had claimed. Rather, she had talked *at* them, which is entirely different. I've seen too many instances where this pattern of communication has led to lying and deception. When parents are dogmatic, children respond not to the message itself but to the manner of delivery. They perceive dictatorial communication as condescending, which it is.

So I said, "Carol, I'm concerned that if you speak too harshly to your children, they'll miss the message you want them to learn, and they'll spend their energies trying to figure out how to beat the system."

"Are you saying I should just let them do what they want?" she asked.

"Not exactly. But I am suggesting that you focus on a larger issue. Rather than trying to force them to do exactly as you say, you have an opportunity to guide their thinking. You can teach them how to process ideas for themselves."

"But if I do that, they might make the wrong decisions," Carol protested. "I don't want them to think that those weird rock groups are acceptable heroes for them to imitate."

"I share your concern, Carol. But I'm thinking about all those times your kids are going to have to make moral decisions when you're not there to give them the right answers."

Learning to let go of imperative thinking in parenting can be tricky. Because children cannot always be trusted to do things in their own best interests, parents face the task of guiding their decisions so problems will not get out of hand.

Because they obviously know more, many adults falsely assume it is necessary—and even good—to be commanding when communicating principles and rules. For a while they may manage to maintain control, but in most cases controlling parents reach a point of despair and disillusionment. Children were not created for enslavement, and when parents allow them little or no freedom, their natural response is to rebel.

My experience tells me that children who are excessively controlled by their parents are prone to major emotional and relational problems. Those problems may manifest themselves during the developmental years (hitting a peak in adolescence), yet they often are not evident until the adult years. The likelihood of rebellion against imperative parenting increases as the son or daughter gains a greater capacity for free thinking. In the toddler and pre-adolescent years, parents at least have the "advantage" of greater reasoning. But beginning in adolescence and extending into adulthood, the parents' ability to maintain rigid control decreases significantly. It is in these years that the deficiencies of imperative parenting are most clearly evidenced.

When counseling with imperative parents, I have found it helpful to emphasize that the long-range goal of parenting is to render their authority unnecessary. I never mean to suggest that parents themselves should eventually be considered unimportant. But it is a fact that one day the parent will be less involved in the child's daily life. The parents who have made themselves indispensable, who refuse to train the child to think for himself, are doing their offspring no favors. Just as my goal in a counseling case is to work myself out of a job, parents have the task of eventually rendering themselves unnecessary as authority figures.

Focusing on Parenting's Ultimate Goal

If we observed a majority of parents, we could conclude that the major goal of parenting is conformity. Most parents, guided by imperative thinking, give high priority to fitting their child into a prescribed mold. The net result is temporary cooperation without a deeply established habit of reasoning. Yet parents are successful when they train their children to consider options and arrive at their own conclusions about major decisions.

When I talked to Carol about *her* parenting goal, I could see that she felt uncomfortable.

"I know my children need to learn to think for themselves, Les, but I'm just afraid to trust them with deci-

1. We grant freedom in graduated amounts.

2. We offer choices as often as possible.

3. We realize that telling is not the same as commanding.

4. We openly explore our emotions.

5. We establish equality.

sions that could affect their whole lives. I feel that I *have* to make some decisions for them."

"I'm not saying you shouldn't set restrictions, Carol, but I am suggesting that you need to show them some respect if you expect to get any in return. Instead of telling them what they'd better do, you might *talk* with them about your beliefs and ask them about theirs."

"I'd like to try," she said. "Can you give me some suggestions on how to get started?"

"You could try telling them something like, "I'm sure you've noticed that your friends' parents let them watch TV videos that we don't watch in our home. People have different likes and dislikes, and that's their privilege. But you know that I've always wanted you to be exposed to the right influences, and I hope you agree that rock videos are not what you could call wholesome. If you do agree, there may be times when you choose to tell your friends how you feel."

"But what if my kids don't respond the way I want them to?" Carol asked. "What then?"

"You can only control what you are capable of controlling," I told her. "You can let them know that the restriction against videos in your home is permanent. That's something you can manage. But don't set them up to lie to you by trying to control everything they do when they're out of your sight. That will increase your frustration, which in the long run will harm your relationship with them even more. Use this as an opportunity to provoke them to think. Ask questions. But don't be so overbearing that they're afraid to be honest with you.

"When major issues of morality and ethics are at stake," I said, "it is certainly appropriate to establish restrictions and consequences. But in doing this there are two rules to remember: (1) Don't throw so many restrictions at them that they eventually tune you out altogether; and (2) let them help create their own restrictions. That way, they will know you are willing to hear their point of view."

To help Carol develop a more flexible style of communicating, I asked her to recall scenes from her own childhood. "Did you ever wish your parents would trust you more?"

"How did you know?" Carol asked with a smile.

"I felt that way myself when I was a kid. Children are very sensitive to how much or how little their parents trust them. When they receive directives from their parents, the implied messages are more important than the immediate issues."

In our next sessions Carol and I talked about the specifics of her style of parenting, with the idea that she would learn how to apply freedom, rather than imperative thinking to her relationship with her children. Five important ideas came out of our discussions.

1. *We Grant Freedom in Graduated Amounts*

It would be preposterous to propose that we give children unlimited freedom from the beginning of life. The ability to live responsibly is dependent on our capacity for inner philosophical guidance. This is a quality that can only be learned through years of instruction by parents and teachers. Therefore parents are responsible for introducing and enforcing structure in the early years, with the idea of delegating more decision making to the child as each year passes.

I explained this to Carol by giving an analogy. I said, "Free people can be like a country dog that can go as he chooses, but learns to stay close to home. That's the ultimate goal of parenting, to teach the child to stay close to good convictions in a world where he is free to do as he chooses. But a child differs from an adult in that he *needs* some structure. Children find security in boundaries."

"So you're not suggesting that my children can do whatever they want."

"That's right. In the beginning, children need parents to set boundaries, making them a little larger each year. It's important to give them increasing permission to think for themselves as they move toward adulthood. When they enter adulthood, parents can bring the fences down altogether."

Carol admitted that she had not given much thought to the idea of slowly, but surely, transferring decision making to her children. She had been so consumed with making them conform that short-term goals had taken priority over long-range considerations.

To begin developing a "big picture" approach to parenting, it is helpful for each parent to take a close look at the way he or she communicates with the children. Ask yourself the following questions:

- "When I talk to my child, am I looking out for his future, or for my own immediate interests?"
- "Does my discipline style build character in the child?"
- "Do I speak *with* the child or talk *to* him?"
- "Does the child understand my reasoning?"
- "Do I encourage in-depth thinking?"
- "Am I communicating with the child on a higher level than a year ago?"

Once you are committed to giving your child increasing freedom as he becomes capable of handling it responsibly, you can begin introducing him to the decision process involved in making choices.

2. *We Offer Choices as Often as Possible*

Freedom and choices go hand in hand. Parents operating from a free mindset recognize that they are helping the child mature when they allow him to examine his options. Early in life, these options are minor: which cereal to eat, which color dress to wear. Then as the years progress the choices will relate to more complex issues: what to do with sibling conflict, how to handle awkward social situations, how to communicate convictions. In each case, the parent is guided by the thought, *I could simply tell my child what to do, but I'd rather teach him how to think.*

Carol had complained about frequent tensions related to problems Lana was having with one of her girlfriends. The friend was encouraging Lana to spend money on cheap jewelry, and Carol was upset because Lana was being easily influenced. Arguments erupted when she wasn't able to make Lana act as she wanted.

"I've tried to tell Lana that she's got to use more common sense," Carol told me, "but my words just seem to go in one ear and out the other. I get so frustrated I could scream."

"How does Lana respond when you encourage her to make her own decision?" I asked.

Carol's face looked blank. "I guess I've never really told her she could solve the problem on her own. I'm not sure I'd feel comfortable doing that."

"But you feel frustrated being a fix-it person every time Lana has a problem. Why not just step out of the picture and put the problem solving in her lap?"

Carol liked the sound of this. "How exactly would I do this?"

"You can begin by letting your daughter know she has a limited amount of money to spend each week," I said. "Let her know she has some leeway in the way she spends it; then let her learn that spending too much money on one item leaves her less to spend on another.

"As her parent, you wish she could have a mistake-free childhood. Yet it's inevitable that she'll make some errors along the way. I'm suggesting that you be a facilitator, not a problem solver. After you help her understand the options and consequences, you can back off and let her decide which way she'll go. These small experiences will teach her more than a hundred lectures."

When we regularly explore options with our children, we are preparing them to handle future freedom with reason. Additionally, we are freeing ourselves from the impossibility of making decisions for someone who ultimately cannot be held under our control.

3. *We Realize That Telling Is Not the Same as Commanding*

Children cannot necessarily be trusted to make reasonable decisions on their own. This is not to say that children can *never* be trusted. I simply imply that instructions are sometimes necessary to keep children grounded in common sense. For example, most teenagers would prefer to stay out later at night than their parents deem reasonable. In cases like these, parental instruction is required.

Unfortunately, too many parents become commanding. They often take the need for instruction as a license to dictate. It is hard for a child not to take offense when his parent is being condescending—even if he knows the parent is right.

"My son, Keith, has been arguing with me lately about doing his homework," Carol said. "When he comes home from school, I let him relax and play until supper time. Then after supper he has to finish his homework before he can do anything else. But lately I've had a hard time making him understand what he's supposed to do."

"Your schedule for him sounds reasonable enough," I said. "How does the problem tend to unfold?"

"When we finish supper, he wants to play his computer games. I tell him that he's just putting off his homework, and he's *got* to get it done now. He doesn't like it one bit."

"Does he talk back to you?"

"Oh yes! He's got a sharp tongue," said Carol. "Sometimes we've both said some pretty harsh words and ended up mad at each other. I've explained to him over and over how he can't expect to do well in school if he refuses to do his homework. He's just got to understand that I won't tolerate his insubordination."

"It seems that you've gone beyond the point of just telling him what you want him to do," I suggested. "Instead, you get pulled into a power play where your communication becomes very commanding. This is where you begin losing ground."

"I know that's true," said Carol, "because I often feel like he doesn't care what I think. But how can I handle it differently?"

"The first rule of thumb is to refrain from commanding speech," I explained. "The more you try to coerce him, the less real authority you have. Subconsciously he's thinking, *If Mom is having to work so hard at making me see things her way, maybe she's not sure about what she's saying. I think I'll try challenging her to see if I can find a crack in her armor.*

Carol smiled as she said, "You must be a mind reader because I've felt like he's been saying that very thing to me. I'm getting tired of trying to convince him that I know what's best for him."

"Then don't try any more. You can't do his thinking for him. Let him decide how he feels about your rules. Stick to your convictions but don't talk about them all the time."

"So when I tell him to get started on his homework and he balks, I shouldn't argue with him?"

"That's right. Let him see that you are so confident that you don't need to back up your suggestions with arm-twisting. Simply tell him; don't plead with him."

"Okay, so I won't twist his arm. But what if he still won't do his homework?"

"That's when you explain the consequences to him. Make sure your tone of voice isn't coercive. Just be matter-of-fact. Then make sure you follow through on the consequences if you have to."

When parents are commanding, children feel trapped. This eventually feeds either rebelliousness or depression. Parameters can still be maintained by way of consequences, but the difference is that the parent is trying to guide the child, not think for him.

Patience is required as we learn to drop our imperative style of speech. Often children will continue to try to "put hooks" in their parents, prodding them into an argument. At this point, we can refuse to offer a rebuttal, letting our instructions stand pat, or we can gently and firmly repeat the instructions. As it becomes obvious that we are not going to be defensive, the child slowly realizes on his own that his protests are useless.

4. *We Openly Explore Our Emotions*

Imperative parents insist upon fitting their children into neat, predictable packages. They emphasize performance, since performance can be programmed. Imperative parents tend to shy away from emotional issues because emotions can be unpredictable. They would best be forgotten, it seems, or at least minimized.

When we become committed to freedom, we realize that emotions are part of what we are. We may not always enjoy the emotions being expressed, yet we realize it is unhealthy to pretend they don't exist. We are willing to explore emotions. We take time to talk with our children about their feelings, both pleasant and unpleasant. And we allow the children to see that parents have feelings too.

In spite of the fact that Carol was rather emotionally expressive, she admitted that she often felt at a loss when either she or her children expressed strong negative feelings. "My kids don't lack for open displays of affection. Both my husband and I can hug them easily and tell them of our love. But when our kids express negative emotions, it isn't easy to deal with them."

"Whenever a troublesome emotion surfaces, Carol, you don't have to tie it down with a solution immediately. That's the same as saying, 'Get rid of this feeling quick! It's wrong of you to feel this way!'"

Carol nodded. "I guess I do put too much pressure on myself to get things settled right away."

"You initially sought counseling because of your inclination toward tension," I said. "And one of the most tension-producing thoughts is the notion that you have to solve someone else's problems immediately."

"But does it do any good to let my children's emotions just run wild?" she asked.

"Not at all," I responded. "I think you'll find that as you allow a child to feel a negative emotion, it will become less overwhelming. For example, if Lana tells you how anxious she feels about an upcoming test at school, show her some empathy. Say something like, 'I know it's a little nerve-racking to try to remember all the facts in your geography book. This is going to require some real concentration!' You don't have to solve her problem for her. But you can just allow her to be human. That way she'll feel accepted for who she is . . . and that's what she's really looking for."

By attempting to hide from emotions, parents can inadvertently give more energy to a child's feelings than is healthy. Suppressed emotions build up inside and become even more difficult to manage. The more the emotions are suppressed, the more negatively charged they become.

Allowing a child to express his emotions doesn't mean solutions are never discussed, but a base of understanding is established first. Parents show they are receptive, not easily shocked. When parent and child can discuss a problem openly, without fear or embarrassment, it is a lot easier to explore options together.

5. *We Establish Equality*

Parents have a delicate balance to maintain because, while they do indeed know more than children, they do not possess superior worth. Human worth is equal, but it is easy to forget this fact when the imperative mindset insists that worth must be earned. By speaking in strong imperatives, parents can communicate, "I hope you realize that I am of more value than you because I've already proven myself. Now it's up to you!"

Carol was eager to learn how to establish equality with her children and at the same time hold to her position of authority.

"Much of this is related to the way you speak," I told her. "For example, we often sound insulting when we ask questions. Take, for instance, a situation in which your daughter doesn't clean up the kitchen after dinner as you have asked. It's easy to say, 'What did I just ask you to do *ten minutes ago?*' The implied message is, 'You moron!'"

"It is easy to speak like that. I'm afraid I'm pretty good at it. I guess I never thought about what my words made Lana feel like."

"Here's another example," I said. "Let's say your son is trying to decide if he wants to go on an outing with a friend's family. You could say to him, 'I know you can decide what would be best for you. Just let me know when you make up your mind.' In a very simple way you're affirming your trust in him."

"When I was a teenager," Carol said, "a favorite aunt repeatedly told me she was impressed by my responsible nature. I never thought I had done anything special to deserve her compliments, but I felt she trusted and respected me and I was comfortable around her."

The same feeling of comfort and respect gradually developed between Carol and her children as Carol began to build her communications on a new foundation of equality and trust. She discovered that when she granted her children freedom of choice within the limits of the family structure, they began to respond responsibly. Negative emotions still surfaced, but Carol no longer treated them like skeletons in the closet. She was learning that her own tensions lessened in proportion to the freedom she granted others.

CHAPTER 13

Freedom and Christianity

A fairly handsome man in his mid-thirties, Bruce greeted me with a firm handshake that belied the worried look on his face. He spoke affectionately of his nine-year-old son, Peter, and seemed to be happy with his job as ticket agent for an airline. But immediately after his divorce five years ago, he had become sexually promiscuous and had developed the habit of drinking heavily almost every weekend. He sought counseling because, as he put it, he was "tired of so many painful emotions."

He confided that about a year prior to our meeting he had become a Christian and had vowed to clean up his act.

"I grew up in a Baptist church," he said. "At one time I was very active in youth activities and Bible studies. I knew what kind of life I should be leading. A couple of years ago, I was feeling miserable about how empty my life had become. That's when I began going back to church. At first I attended only sporadically, but I realized I wasn't being consistent and stepped up my involvement. After hearing some of the preacher's messages, I realized I wasn't a born-again Christian, so I made a profession of faith in Christ. It really changed my life, and I've stopped trying to be the town roustabout."

"When you called for an appointment, you mentioned something about erratic emotions," I said. "Can you give me an example of the kinds of problems you've been having?"

"I'm too inconsistent," Bruce said. "At times I feel really motivated to live right, but at other times I go right back to some of my old habits, like letting my temper get the best of me. I know as a Christian I'm not supposed to have these kinds of problems. I feel guilty for not measuring up, and sometimes I get depressed because I get so disgusted with myself."

"Did you ever feel like this before you became a Christian?" I asked.

"Well, my temper has always been a problem. In fact, that's part of the reason for my divorce. I've always been pretty stubborn, too, but the guilt and depression are new. For the first time in my life I finally know what right living is all about, but I'm not a good enough Christian to make the grade."

"Strange as it sounds," I reflected, "it seems that your Christian principles may be working against you. I'd like to help you gain some perspective in your spirituality."

Maintaining Freedom as a Christian

A problem commonly arises when Christians attempt to reconcile the absolute truths of Christianity with their own cravings to be in control.

God never intended us to hold a position of ultimate authority over ourselves or anyone else. Yet the idea of lording the absolute truth of Christianity over others is so alluring that many of us find ourselves in positions of false superiority. Likewise, because it is so easy to condemn ourselves for failing to live up to the absolute standards of Christianity, some of us collapse under the weight of false inferiority.

How can we prevent our absolute Christian beliefs from solidifying into a rigid, controlling, imperative mindset? We need to consider the various ways we can maintain freedom as Christians.

God Is Absolute; I Am Not

Only God has the right to be imperative. He alone possesses consummate knowledge, permitting Him to make irrefutable declarations and decisions. Fully sovereign, He is Lord of all that is, and He has final determination in all matters. No one can possibly match His wisdom, a fact that sometimes frustrates those who feel they must have immediate answers to all problems.

The Bible is an extension of the absolute mind of God. Inspired by the Holy Spirit, it is as reliable as God Himself. It offers great guidance in all kinds of relationships. It is pertinent. It has bearing on our daily decisions. Consequently, Christians have learned to turn to its pages for hope and direction. The Bible has become a compass for many who seek the best way to respond to all kinds of circumstances.

It is in the application of God's absolute truth that imperative people create problems, both within themselves and toward others. They reason (often subconsciously) that since God is absolute, they have the same right as God to be absolute in the communication and application of God's Word. They can be so commanding that they appear to others to be "playing God." They assume the right to judge and rule—qualities reserved for God alone. They think, *If the Bible prescribes a way to live, it is my duty to enforce it.* This was never intended by God. He does not need humans to usurp authority that does not belong to them. This was a sub-

ject that I delicately discussed with Bruce. He told me
how frustrated he got when others failed to respect
Christian directives. And he pushed himself so hard to
be the perfect Christian that when he inevitably failed,
he was overcome with unnecessary guilt.

"Bruce," I told him, "if you're experiencing painful
emotions as you try to be true to your conviction that
the Christian way is the best path to a balanced lifestyle, there are two possible explanations. First, either
your Christian ideas really aren't that good after all, or
second, something is at work that is making it hard for
you to live up to your Christian standards."

"Well, the first possibility is out," Bruce replied. "I've
been on the other side of the fence, and I'm convinced
that my Christian principles are the only way to go."

"So that leaves the second possibility. Bruce, I'm getting the feeling that you're trying too hard. You want to
be an exceptional Christian, and there's nothing the
matter with that. But the high standards you set make
you judgmental toward yourself and impatient with
others. You expect life to unfold exactly as the Bible prescribes, and you feel guilty and depressed when you or
anyone else falls short of the mark."

Bruce seemed confused. "I'm not sure I understand,"
he said. "Won't I be disloyal to my beliefs if I become
more lax?"

"Not at all. Think of it this way. An aerospace engineer is required to utilize highly advanced mathemati-
cal equations as he lays out plans for an engine design.
The principles he uses are reliable, verified through
much research. Now imagine how competent you
would feel if I told you to compute some of the equations
for that engineer."

Bruce had to smile. "I wouldn't even know where to
start. The closest I come to aerospace engineering is
when I'm at my job selling airplane tickets."

"On a much larger scale," I said, "God has a high-level, correct equation for each of our lives. It is absolutely purposeful and fully reliable. But it can also seem complex. It's not easy for you or me to implement every aspect of it. By recognizing our limitations, we aren't disagreeing with His absolute will. We are merely acknowledging that we are not God."

"So you're suggesting that my emotions get muddied when I assume I know all the answers, then find out I don't."

I nodded.

In a moment, Bruce said, "It would be a tremendous relief to really accept the fact that I don't have to be as perfect as He is."

"Sanctification is the word used to describe our maturing toward Christ-likeness," I explained. "We'll always want to be aiming for Christianity's lofty goals. The key is not to be so demanding of ourselves or others that we get caught up in negative emotions when we fail to be perfect.

"When we make allowances for human error, it's not the same as condoning sin," I told him. "Rather, it's an acknowledgement of reality.

Christianity Is Faith, Not Rules

It is difficult for some people to understand that Christianity is not a system of rules and regulations. In our childhood, many of us heard so much about the "shalt nots" of the Bible that we grew up thinking of it as a thick, black book full of impossible commandments. If that mindset goes unchallenged, we can live our entire adult lives believing that a Christian is someone who knows he must not stray from the Bible's dogma. This kind of thinking labels Christianity as a weak, legalistic way of life, certainly not a life of freedom.

I asked Bruce to think back to his childhood experiences and share some of his feelings about what growing up was like in his family.

"My family was pretty strict," he told me. "When I was in grade school and high school, I wasn't exposed to much else besides Christian morality. My father was what you might call 'the good kind.' We never saw any alcohol or cigarettes in our house. I wasn't allowed to play cards or go swimming on Sundays because he said he wanted me to set a good example for other kids my age."

"Did your church life revolve around following all the rules, too?" I asked.

"Absolutely. I had to do all the correct things, whether I felt like it or not. But after I left home, church was one of the first things to go by the wayside. By that time, I was ready to have some fun. College was one never-ending party. My parents didn't seem to know what to say about my lifestyle, so the subject was just swept under the rug.

"In my early twenties I married a girl who was a lot like me in the respect that she also had rejected her parents' stodgy ways. We had quite a social life for three years; then our son was born. That slowed us down, and I guess you could say when we finally paused long enough to take inventory of our marriage, there was very little to build on."

"So that's when you got the divorce."

"Right. And then I went right back to my old swinging single's life for another three or four years. Fortunately, I'm finished with all that now, but I've got to admit that I'm disappointed. When I turned to Christianity, I expected to feel peaceful inside, and instead I'm plagued by emotional ups and downs."

"It sounds like you've returned to the same kind of life you grew up with, Bruce. It's easy to turn Christianity into a list of do's and don'ts. But when you do, you can feel crushed under the weight of those heavy regulations, and your emotions will be anything but peaceful."

Many of us try to simplify life by making easy-to-understand, concrete rules. One woman typified this when she told me: "I don't want to philosophize about everything. I just want to know what I'm supposed to do and when I'm supposed to do it." We are all mentally lazy enough that we would rather not be challenged by circumstances that require deliberation and theoretical application. This inclination lends itself to an imperative approach to Christianity, since imperative thinking boils broad issues down to cut-and-dried answers. Thus Christianity becomes to many a concrete, plug-it-in system of ready directives.

That's what was happening to Bruce. He had sought Christianity when he was trying to make sense of his tensions. For a year he had focused on the yes's and no's of Christian living and had found the structure he wanted. But by the time he came to my office, his Christianity was less fulfilling because he had learned that people (family, friends, self) could not always be reduced to his imperative preferences. His emotional fallout was due to an insistence upon fitting his world into a safe, predictable pattern.

Faith Takes Priority Over Good Works

If humans were capable of obeying regulations consistently, God would have gladly allowed Christianity to become a simple list of good deeds. But our inclination toward sin is so pervasive that God instead allowed salvation to be based upon the substitution principle. His own Son, Jesus, did indeed live in full accordance with God's ways. Not only was His external life perfect, but His inner spirit was without flaw. If humans were capa-

ble of following all regulations, Christ's death would
have been unnecessary.

Faith in Christ, then, is far more central to Christianity
than good works. Does this mean that good works are
meaningless? Not at all. They are a reflection of our
commitment to Christ's teachings. But rather than con-
centrating too intently on "doing the job right," Christians find favor with God when they first give over their
lives in faithfulness to Christ, then put that faithfulness
into action.

Bruce had spoken to a minister about the necessity of
living by faith, and he talked about this in my office.
"I'm learning that my dogmatic ideas are inconsistent
with a life of faith in Christ. I know my focus needs to
change."

"When you focus too exclusively on the regulations of
Christianity, the net result is worry and anger and false
guilt," I told him. "Eventually your emotions can be so
burdensome that Christianity can lose its appeal."

"I see what you mean. And when I put more emphasis
on faith, I can feel glad even though I admit my inability
to live perfectly."

"Right. The irony of it all is that when you place more
emphasis on faith, your efforts at doing good works flow
more easily. Also when you respond less legalistically to
others, they'll respond better to you."

In explaining Christianity to the first generation of believers, the apostle Paul underscored how grace is above
the law. Jewish Christians, in particular, were accus-
tomed to doing proper exercises to prove their commitment to God. But Paul recognized that this obsession
with the law detracted from their understanding of
God's gift of unconditional love.

"We are living on a higher plane now," was his message. The law, with its emphasis on correct works, con-
tinues to be good. But grace, with its emphasis on

receiving the unearned gift of forgiveness, is better. It leads us to examine higher truths than the law. Instead of being carried away with technicalities, we can focus on such positive internal qualities as peace, love, and joy, which are by-products of faith.

Worship Takes First Priority

Since the imperative mindset is more focused on performance than on relational qualities, the Christian guided by imperative thinking will be more consumed with what he is supposed to be doing than with loving God.

Have you ever tried to conjure up a mental picture of heaven? I rarely think of it as a place where the saints will be waiting to applaud me for my good deeds. Instead, I see myself praising God—singing and shouting, visibly expressing my adoration for the Almighty. I envision myself in a perfect relationship with Him.

If heaven is such a place of relating, should we wait until we get there to begin the process of responding in that way to God? Not at all. We Christians can find great joy now by pouring our energies into worship of God. Rather than viewing Him as a stern taskmaster who will crack the whip when one of His subjects gets out of line, we can think of Him as an approachable figure who is keenly interested in our emotions, who feels sorrow when we are in pain and joy when we are happy.

As I came to understand how Bruce had placed more emphasis on Christian performance than on relating with God, I said to him, "Bruce, it's no wonder that Christianity has become burdensome to you. You seem to have forgotten that faith is based on a special relationship with God. When you focus more intensely on the relational aspect of your spiritual life, performances will still follow, but they will be an extension of love rather than duty."

"I really want that," Bruce said. "When I first became a Christian, the idea of God's grace appealed to me. But somehow I began paying more attention to the importance of works."

"The Bible says quite a bit about being free when we accept Christ," I said. "That freedom comes when we realize that God *wants* to love us even though our performances may be poor. Our job as Christians is to receive that love daily."

"Just this week I was reading about the prodigal son," Bruce said. "I was impressed with how much his father loved him no matter what had happened in his past. The elder brother couldn't comprehend their father's love, and he lost out on the gift that was offered. It dawned on me that I didn't want to be like the elder brother, so intent on doing everything right that he couldn't receive his father's blessings."

When worship of God takes priority over sheer performance, major changes occur. Bruce found that church became a place where worship was the prime directive. He was able to see that his Bible study classes could be opportunities to draw closer to God through cooperative study and sharing of ideas, rather than just evenings set aside for intellectual discussions. He began to include expressions of joy, adoration, and thanksgiving in his prayers. He found new meaning in the words, "Love the Lord your God with all your heart and with all your soul and with all your mind. . . . And . . . love your neighbor as yourself."[1] Bruce grew to see that his love for God could be made manifest in human relations.

Beliefs Are Based on More than Just Tradition

Imperative thinking prompts individuals to attempt to package life into neat bundles. Freedom, however, allows for a broad array of options. This is, of course, the point I have been making throughout this book. It is well worth repeating, for it applies to all beliefs and moral values.

Prior to his return to Christianity, Bruce's life had been very undisciplined. He had been susceptible to spur-of-the-moment dares. He had not respected authority. He wanted no accountability. The result was disarray in relationships that might otherwise have been rewarding and inconsistencies in his emotions and commitments. By the time he considered the lifestyle of Christianity, he was ready for some needed regimentation.

I spoke with him about this. "Actually, Bruce, your commitment to Christianity came at a good time for you. Had you continued in your old lifestyle, you'd be an emotional wreck. Your new life has given you some good guidance. It's provided you with a set of beliefs that protect you from empty worldliness."

A look of uncertainty crossed his face. "I agree. That's why I can't understand why my emotions have been so painful in the last couple of months. I thought I was supposed to be uplifted, not hindered, by being a Christian."

"I suspect that you quickly learned what a good Christian is *supposed* to act like, and you set out to fit the mold. Also you had memories from your childhood about the Christian lifestyle you were forced to live then. You adopted those, assuming that your parents must have been right."

"That's exactly what happened," Bruce admitted. "I guess I didn't know I could have the luxury of questioning the status quo."

"I'm not trying to turn you into a skeptic," I assured him. "But I am suggesting that you can feel trapped by your beliefs if you've simply adopted them because someone else told you to."

"In other words," Bruce responded, "if I'm going to

commit my whole life to God's absolutes, I need to be certain that these are my beliefs." He nodded his head slowly as the idea took root.

"Let me give you an example," I said. "I believe the principle of forgiveness is a solid instruction. But before I decide to forgive someone, I can ask myself: *Why do I want to do this? What difference does it make? What might happen if I choose to hold a grudge instead?* Ultimately I'll forgive someone because I've given full consideration to all the options, and it is the one I prefer."

"I can see how this could apply to my outlook on morality. In the past year I've abstained from sexual immorality and alcohol consumption because I felt I had to do that to be accepted as a Christian, but you're suggesting that I should dig deeper and learn for myself why these behaviors would be pleasing to the Lord."

"That's what I'm suggesting," I said. "You'll have greater emotional composure when your Christianity is based on your own convictions from God, rather than from an outside source. You'll probably maintain very similar behavior, but your motivation will be entirely different. It will be internal, rather than external."

After the resurrection of Christ, a new gift was offered to believers, something never before available. It was the indwelling presence of the Holy Spirit. Teachings from men and long-held traditions can still be given high priority, but they are filtered through personal convictions arising from the Holy Spirit's prompting.

Humanness Is Still Allowed

Some people assume that *real* Christians should *never* have problems. Or at least their difficulties should be minor ones. Only the backslidden or unsaved are susceptible to insecurity or depression, so they think. Therefore, many Christians will expend enormous efforts attempting to appear "together" when in fact they are not. Ironically, this denial of problems increases the likelihood for major emotional tension and worse problems.

Unfortunately, some Christians do judge those who reveal their humanness. They try to patch up these people, quickly, or they refuse fellowship with them altogether. Therefore some Christians like Bruce get caught in the impossible task of trying to live a perfect life. These people lose the joy of the Christian experience. Some lose most of their motivation. That had not yet happened to Bruce, but if he did not reverse his imperative approach to Christianity, it would only be a matter of time.

In one of our discussions, Bruce conveyed a frustrating experience that had happened just two days before. "I told my prayer group that I had sought counseling because of some depressing and confused emotions. I was disappointed by the way some of the people responded."

"I can only imagine what you might have heard," I said. "Some people think Christians really don't need to get counseling, that their faith should be enough to ease their burdens."

"Fortunately no one criticized counseling per se," he told me. "Instead I got a barrage of advice. One person told me I needed to spend more time on my knees in prayer. Another said I had to go back and talk to my former wife about all our problems. Someone else gave me the names of some books I should read. It's not that I totally disagreed with their ideas, but that's not what I needed."

"You were simply looking for some emotional support, weren't you?"

Bruce nodded.

"I can tell by their willingness to offer advice that they care about you, but apparently your humanness was threatening to them. They hurried to sweep it under the rug."

Bruce spoke calmly. "Maybe they don't realize it, but if they'd just said something like, 'Yeah, I've felt the same way myself,' I'd have felt more encouraged."

Some Christian groups do not always freely acknowledge our human frailties. Even so, we do not have to become guarded in our social interactions. We may choose to use discretion with certain people, but we don't ever have to resort to a phony denial that we have problems. To experience the freedom of Christianity, we need people who can serve as outlets for our emotional experiences. People like Bruce will do well to search out healthy support groups that will allow for human failings.

The apostle Peter pointed his flock to God's original plan for humankind when he wrote, "Bear one another's burdens, and so fulfill the law of Christ."[2] The law of Christ is to reflect the love of God even as we point others toward holiness.

The gift of free choice allows us to decide how we will expend our energies in becoming the kind of people God intended us to be. Any brand of imperative thinking or living detracts from the possibility of our fulfillment. The seductions of negative thoughts are legion, the temptation to control is a strong one. But freedom, as God's gift to us, is a great truth. It is our option to claim it as our inheritance. The choice is ours.

Endnotes

Chapter 7   Do You Have an Inborn Craving for Control?
1. Isaiah 53:6.

Chapter 9   Choosing to Walk Humbly
1. Micah 6:8 (NKJV).
2. Micah 7:19 (NKJV).

Chapter 10   Choosing to Be Content
1. Philippians 4:12–13.

Chapter 13   Freedom and Christianity
1. Matthew 22:37–39.
2. Galatians 6:2 (NKJV).

About the Author

Dr. Les Carter is a nationally known expert in the field of Christian counseling with more than fifteen years of private practice. He is a psychotherapist with the Minirth-Meier Clinic and is a weekly guest on the clinic's popular radio program, "The Minirth-Meier Clinic," heard daily on the Moody Broadcasting Network. Dr. Carter is the author of seven other books, including *Putting the Past Behind, Good 'N' Angry, The Missing Peace,* and *The Prodigal Spouse.* A popular speaker, he leads seminars in cities across the United States.

Carter earned his B.A. from Baylor University and his M.Ed. and Ph.D. from North Texas State University. He and his family currently live in Dallas, Texas.